STUDIES IN ENGLISH LITERATURE

Volume XVIII

THE SPIRITUAL BASIS

OF

PIERS PLOWMAN

by

EDWARD VASTA

1965

MOUTON & CO.

LONDON · THE HAGUE · PARIS

Printed in The Netherlands by Mouton & Co., Printers, The Hague.

To My Parents

ACKNOWLEDGEMENTS

Since this study of *Piers Plowman* has its roots in graduate work begun ten years ago, and indirectly goes back even to my first confrontation with *Piers* in an undergraduate course taught by Professor Rufus Rauch at Notre Dame, it is impossible to acknowledge all contributors. I can only acknowledge those whose contribution was direct, and ask others to accept my thanks for their assistance.

No one has assisted me more than Professor Robert W. Ackerman of the English Department of Stanford University. His interest and assistance extended from a seminar in *Piers Plowman* to the Ph. D. dissertation that followed, and then to this book that followed after. To him I express my lasting gratitude.

My thanks also to those who gave assistance along the way: to Professor John T. Frederick, former Head of the English Department at Notre Dame, and to Professor Alvan S. Ryan, present Head, for their encouragement and their special consideration in removing obstacles to my work; to Mrs. John R. Marvin and Dr. Francis D. Lazenby, both of the Notre Dame Library, for their personal efforts in securing materials; to the readers of this study in its dissertation form at Stanford; Professor Edwin M. Good of the Department of Theology, and Professor Lawrence V. Ryan, Director of the Graduate Program in Humanities; and finally to Professor Mortimer Donovan of Notre Dame's English Department, who gave my manuscript a colleague's reading and me a colleague's offering of his knowledge and wisdom.

Thanks also to the editors of *Philological Quarterly* for permission to incorporate in this book arguments they published in an article.

Finally, to the Danforth Foundation, the Ford Foundation, Stanford University, and the University of Notre Dame, thanks for myself and for my family. These institutions provided the hard necessities of time and money, and in ample amounts. In the measure of their gifts they made an immeasurable contribution to the inception, completion, and publication of this book.

E. V.

TABLE OF CONTENTS

I. ISSUES AND APPROACHES

Seventy-five years and more have passed since Skeat's three-text edition inaugurated the "modern" era of *Piers Plowman* scholarship; yet in all that time, as in centuries preceding, no fundamental interpretation, basic outline, or essential perspective has conduced to a reasonably complete and widely accepted explication of Langland's poem. The early view that *Piers* is a series of social vignettes has produced no substantial study, while the current view that *Piers* is unified by the quest for salvation has produced a multitude of studies noted for their variety of interpretations and approaches. Some say the poem unfolds Langland's personal quest for salvation; others, the quest every individual must pursue; still others, the quest for the salvation of society. Governing issues have been defined as the use of *temporalia* and the value of learning, the three kinds of lives Christians may live, or the divine aids which come from the Trinity to man. Again, as a poem involving salvation, *Piers* has been read as a biographical allegory, a moral allegory, a social allegory, a polysemous allegory conducted on three continuous levels, a mixture of these, and as not an allegory at all. The critical methods employed range from the "new critical" on one end to the exegetical on the other. The total result thus far has been a diversity of independent studies, intersecting at many points, but never converging to shed steady light.

Some significant progress has undoubtedly been made, however, although it falls short of fundamental understanding of the poem as a whole. For one thing, disagreement has promoted increasingly more meticulous research into relevant background material, and increasingly more detailed analysis of the literal meaning of scenes and passages. While early criticism tends to be imaginative but general, sometimes sweeping, recent works, including such ill received studies as Robertson's and Huppé's *Piers Plowman and Scriptural Tradition*, have thrown significant light on the literal meaning of many of the poem's smaller parts. Or again, most interpretations offered thus far, involving such basic notions as the sanctity of labor, the practical nature of the poem's teaching, its autobiographical immediacy, and the governing issues mentioned above, have failed to rally scholarship around them, but have nevertheless validly directed attention to important aspects of the poem. A satisfactory interpretation will very likely modify and integrate these notions rather than reject them outright.

The most important sign of progress, however, is that more and more scholars are coming to feel that *Piers Plowman* must be read in the light of medieval spirituality. Langland has been persistently associated with spiritual writers, and although scholars do not agree in what respects and to what extent his work belongs among the works of mystics, that there is an important connection is nowadays being openly argued. This recurring view, in fact, while as yet undeveloped, constitutes the single most enduring "tradition" one may find in *Piers Plowman* studies, thus suggesting by its very persistence that herein may lie the true basis for understanding the poem. More significant is that this "tradition" evokes with increasing urgency the question of whether *Piers* deals with the mystic's way of salvation – the way of the perfect – or that of the ordinary Christian. It insists, in other words, on specifying the currently accepted quest-for-salvation view by defining how Langland conceives of his goal and the means to it. The notion of salvation in itself is unworkably vague and general, embracing multitudinous issues involving, especially in the Middle Ages, practically every aspect of life. Having remained unspecified, the current view merely circumscribes a vast general context for the poem rather than positing a focal point from which knowledge may expand. The primary reason for the present diversity of interpretations is this failure to establish at the outset, precisely and convincingly, the specific nature of the

Dreamer's quest. One of the most significant facts about studies interested in the poem's spirituality is that they call attention to, and invite a solution of, what has been the problem in *Piers Plowman* scholarship all along.

My aim in this study is to respond to the question evoked by this scholarly "tradition": that is, to define the nature of salvation in Langland. I also wish to extend this "tradition" by showing that Langland's goal is, indeed, the goal of the mystic: the quest in this life for "the real but supernatural union between the soul, with its powers of knowledge and love, and God".[1]

The "tradition" I wish to extend begins with J. J. Jusserand, who describes *Piers* as a series of social vignettes, but charged with the intense piety and reformist zeal characteristic of the mystical temperament.[2] The simple observations Jusserand makes, including, for example, that like many mystics Langland is a visionary, are of limited use; but they are not unevocative.[3] The similarities he sees between Langland and the "prophets and prophetesses", as Jusserand calls the group including St. Hildegard and St. Elizabeth of Schoenau in the 12th century, and Matilda of Madgeburg, Henry Suso, and Rulman Merswin in the 14th, are particularly striking and may lead to rich insights. If we take "prophet" in its Old Testament sense (excluding, of course, the notion of being divinely inspired) as designating those who prognosticate, record morally significant historial events, interpret the practices and institutions of this world as they are related to God's will, and urge contemporaries to moral and religious reform, the "prophetic" character of Langland's mind is everywhere manifest in his poem. All the material found in *Piers Plowman* comes under these four ways in which the "prophetic" mind operates, thus suggesting a unifying basis beneath the poem's seemingly digressionary contents. All three versions of *Piers*, furthermore, are the product of this kind of mind, thereby suggesting as well a singularity of authorship. Jusserand does

---

[1] David Knowles's definition of the essence of mysticism in *The English Mystical Tradition* (New York, 1961), p. 21.
[2] *Piers Plowman, A Contribution to the History of English Mysticism*, trans. by M. E. R. (London, 1894).
[3] See especially pp. 192-220.

not use "prophet" in the sense I have just used, but in pointing
to other similarly inclined mystics he notes an historical precedent and a possibly fruitful body of information for characterizing
the mind behind this poem. At any rate, Jusserand evokes a
possibility worth exploring, and that Morton W. Bloomfield,
as we shall see later, has very recently explored, though in a
direction different from that which I or Jusserand have suggested.

Proponents of the three-lives interpretation do not relate
Piers to medieval spirituality explicitly, yet they imply a relationship more fundamental than that defined by Jusserand. Of the
three lives, the Active, Contemplative, and Mixed, the last two
belong exclusively to those in a state of perfection. Any discussion
of these lives, especially the last two, inevitably leads back to
spiritual theology, although neither Wells, Coghill, nor R. W.
Chambers puts the matter in its proper context, and even seem
hardly aware of where their view leads. Indeed, their entire contribution tends to be imaginative and general, confined to what
Wells calls the poem's "larger contours of form",[4] and what
Coghill calls "the larger architectural survey of the poem".[5] Their
propensity to generalize rather than specify is one reason for the
recent overthrow of their interpretation. Under the close scrutiny
of R. W. Frank, Jr.[6] and S. S. Hussey,[7] the three-lives view
seems to fall apart. But there is no question that these three
lives are explicitly involved in the poem, although not necessarily
as governing its structure, and neither Frank nor Hussey has
adequately defined and analyzed their nature. A thorough examination of this whole problem will likely show the three-lives
view to be off-center and over-simplified rather than completely
irrelevant.

Greta Hort's *Piers Plowman and Contemporary Religious
Thought* (London, n. d.)[8] is the first detailed and substantial study

---

[4] "The Construction of *Piers Plowman*", *PMLA*, XLIV (1929), p. 132.
[5] *The Pardon of Piers Plowman*, Sir Israel Gollancz Memorial Lecture,
British Academy (London, 1945), p. 17.
[6] *Piers Plowman and the Scheme of Salvation: An Interpretation of
Dowel, Dobet, and Dobest* (New Haven, 1957), pp. 6-11.
[7] "Langland, Hilton, and the Three Lives", *RES*, n.s., VII (1956), 132-51.
[8] I believe this work was published in 1937.

we have among those which associate *Piers* with mystics and mystical theology.[9] Of weighty importance are Miss Hort's argument that the poem is strictly theological rather than philosophical or devotional, her analysis of its psychology in the light of theological discussions during the Middle Ages, and her coming to the brink of such specifically mystical concepts as the doctrine of deification.[10] One may disagree with her arguments in each of these cases, but one ought not, as seems to have been generally the case, ignore the groundwork she has laid. Had it been followed up, her approach – which is essentially to take Langland's theology seriously – might have been fruitful. While my own study does not utilize Greta Hort's analysis, it is very much in the same spirit, and in one sense extends her view by moving directly into the realm of spirituality rather than stopping at the boundaries. Her description of *Piers* as an *itinerarium mentis in Deum*,[11] for example, would be thoroughly accurate in my view if Miss Hort did not use this mystical formula to mean the mind's reason grappling with theological problems instead of the soul's total development toward perfection and final confrontation with God.

Similarly important, but far less developed than Miss Hort's, are the suggestions made by both E. Talbot Donaldson [12] and Howard Meroney [13] that *Piers* is ultimately concerned with the mystic's way of salvation rather than that of the average Christian. Donaldson suggests that the *Visio* concerns salvation and the *Vita* perfection, and that St. Bernard's concepts of humility, charity, and unity are applicable to the three parts of the *Vita*. But since he is not primarily concerned with interpreting the poem, Donaldson expresses his view summarily. In the same way Meroney, as part of his argument that the A-version is a redaction of B, expresses the view that the *Visio* is ascetic and the *Vita* is mystical, the

[9] T. P. Dunning's *Piers Plowman: An Interpretation of the A-Text* (New York, 1937), is actually the first substantial study of the poem, but does not belong in the "tradition" I am here tracing.
[10] See Hort, *op. cit.*, pp. 81, 115.
[11] *Ibid.*, p. 63.
[12] *Piers Plowman: The C-Text and Its Poet* (New Haven, 1949), ch. VI.
[13] "The Life and Death of Long Wille", *ELH*, XVII (1950), 1-35.

latter dealing in order with the Purgative, Illuminative, and
Unitive stages. His view complements Donaldson's in many ways
– and is given equally brief expression. But both are valuable.
I cannot separate the *Visio* from the *Vita* as distinctly as they
do, since I believe the mystical goal is sought from the outset of
the poem, and while I accept their tripartite terminology, I cannot apply it patly to the three parts of the *Vita*. Nevertheless,
their general conception of the poem finds considerable support
in my own study.

At this point must be mentioned the work of D. W. Robertson,
Jr. and Bernard F. Huppé,[14] not only because their attempt to
analyze *Piers* through the use of medieval exegetical treatises
involves spirituality as well as morality and dogma, and also
re-iterates the three-lives interpretation of the *Vita*, but especially
because the controversy they have aroused has stimulated more
intense interest in the literal meaning of the poem than has
heretofore existed. Critics of Robertson and Huppé have com-
plained about their failure to understand the precise meaning
of theological and philosophical concepts as developed in the
Middle Ages, and to arrive at and hold to the literal meaning of
certain passages in Langland. Even the praise they have received
has been for the light they throw on the literal meaning of
the poem, praise that, in view of their intention to demonstrate
the use of the four-fold method of composition, is in itself
damning. One final result, however, has been the clearing away
of all inhibitions about taking Langland seriously on the literal
level, a wholesome result that makes Robertson's and Huppé's
book a turning point in *Piers Plowman* scholarship. Reaction
against their study, I am convinced, also has contributed to a
climate of acceptance for Frank's claim that *Piers* is to be read
only literally.[15] Frank goes too far in the other direction, I feel.

---

[14] *Piers Plowman and Scriptural Tradition* (Princeton, 1951).
[15] *Op. cit.,* pp. 2-3. See also Frank's "The Art of Reading Medieval
Personification-Allegory", *ELH,* XX (1953), 237-50. Frank describes Piers
as a "personification allegory", but explains that names of personifications
have a literal meaning, and the actions of personified figures dramatize
the nature of the abstraction signified by the literal name. In effect, therefore, *Piers* is not an allegory in the true sense, involving an ostensible

Piers Plowman is indeed an allegory, dramatizing the soul's journey to mystical union with God.

During the past decade, interest in Langland's spirituality has intensified, although it has not yet issued in a satisfactory analysis of the poem, or even in a sufficiently developed basis for a full interpretation. The work of this decade includes those of two German scholars: Helmut Maisack, who in 1953 attempted to place *Piers Plowman* in the context of Cistercian mysticism; and Willy Erzgräber, who four years later interpreted the C-text from the point of view of the general spiritual milieu of the time. Erzgräber, however, denies a development in the poem along specifically mystical lines, affirming instead its concern with problems affecting Christians generally.[16]

Scholars in England and the United States have been especially active. In 1956 T. P. Dunning called for an interpretation of the B-version in terms of the interior regeneration of the individual.[17] By emphasizing the essential interiority of spiritual life, Father Dunning, in effect, calls for a strict application of spiritual psychology: the combination of theology and anthropology that constitutes the core of spiritual teaching. The following year J. J. Lawlor seconded Father Dunning's suggestion, although Lawlor's special interest is in the imaginative elements by which

---

meaning under which lies a "hidden" meaning. David Fowler, *Piers Plowman: Literary Relations of the A and B Text* (Seattle, 1961), agrees with Frank in this and many other respects. Incidentally, both Frank and Fowler reject altogether any structural function of the three lives and do not include mystical aspirations in the poem's scheme of salvation. Thus neither work participates in the "tradition" I am recording.

[16] Helmut Maisack, *William Langlands Verhältnis zum Zisterziensischen Mönchtum: Eine Untersuchung der Vita im Piers Plowman.* Tübingen inaugural Diss. (Balingen, 1953). Willi Erzgräber, *William Langlands Piers Plowman (Eine Interpretation des C-Textes)* (= *Frankfurter Arbeiten aus dem Gebiete der Anglistik und der Amerika-Studien,* III) (Heidelberg, 1957). For information about these two works I am grateful to Dennis V. Moran and his paper, "A Review of *Piers Plowman* Scholarship (1939-1962)", written for a graduate course at Stanford University. Since I have not read these works first hand, my comment on them is brief.

[17] "The Structure of the B-Text of *Piers Plowman*", *RES*, n.s., VII (1956), 225-37.

Langland develops the soul's quest for spiritual perfection.[18] In 1958 Elizabeth Zeeman (Salter) similarly called for an application of subjective spirituality, the mystical process itself, and argued further that the way to mystical union is outlined in Piers's Highway to Truth.[19] In the same year, Conrad Pepler [20] discussed Langland's poem as showing "the way to a first conversion in the midst of social upheaval and unrest",[21] the first conversion that looks forward to spiritual perfection and contemplation. Father Pepler's view of the poem is ambiguously expressed, however, in that he seems to regard *Piers* as dealing only with the first stage of spiritual regeneration, yet describes it as "a practical application of the traditional division of human life into *incipientes, proficientes et perfecti*", the nature of each of these being discussed respectively in *Dowel, Dobet,* and *Dobest*.[22] It would seem, therefore, that only the *Visio* deals with conversion while the *Vita* deals with the remaining three stages in the life of spiritual perfection; but then Father Pepler adds, "We may therefore summarise the Vision thus: Sin, Conversion, and Entry into the first of the Three Lives or Ways." [23] The ambiguity is compounded by Father Pepler's ranging over the entire poem rather than developing a coherent argument, and by his interest in illuminating abstract spiritual problems more than the poem's

[18]   "The Imaginative Unity of Piers Plowman", *RES,* N.s., VIII (1957), 113-26. This article continues the view Lawlor expressed in *"Piers Plowman:* The Pardon Reconsidered", *Modern Language Review,* XLV (1950), 449-458. John Lawlor's fullest development of his view, together with excellent essays on various aspects of the poem, are to be found in his book, *Piers Plowman: An Essay in Criticism* (New York, 1962).
[19]   "Piers Plowman and the Pilgrimage to Truth", *Essays and Studies,* n.s., XI (1958), 1-16. See also her excellent little book in which she expands her discussion: Elizabeth Salter, *Piers Plowman: An Introduction* (Cambridge, Mass., 1962), pp. 81-105.
[20]   *The English Religious Heritage* (St. Louis, 1958), pp. 40-64. Pepler's discussion first appeared in four articles published in *Life of the Spirit,* I (1946-47). "Conversion in Langland", pp. 136-41; "The Beginning of the Way", pp. 101-105; "The Way Opens", pp. 169-72; "Langland's Way to Unity", pp. 198-204.
[21]   *Ibid.,* p. 39.
[22]   *Ibid.,* p. 41.
[23]   *Ibid.*

meaning and structure. Nor is his belief that *Piers* is essentially a work of spirituality more than an assumption.

The scholarly "tradition" I am tracing extends to Morton W. Bloomfield's *Piers Plowman as a Fourteenth-Century Apocalypse* (New Brunswick, New Jersey, n. d., but published in 1962),[24] whose thesis is that *Piers* is concerned with Christian perfection rather than salvation. But Bloomfield rejects the view that *Piers* dramatizes "the odyssey of a mystic towards God",[25] designating as true mystics only those who stressed individual perfection, and argues instead that Langland's search is for social perfection, the regeneration of the whole society. This search, which Bloomfield says ends without success, is the fundamental theme of the poem and makes *Piers Plowman* an essentially apocalyptic work in the pre-12th century monastic tradition rather than a mystical work in the spiritual tradition that flourished from the 12th to the 14th centuries and beyond. Bloomfield develops his thesis by reconstructing Langland's intellectual and artistic milieu and by interpreting a series of supporting passages in the poem. He characterizes his study as "fundamentally an essay in intellectual history and its application to the general comprehension of a work of art".[26]

The presence of apocalyptic elements in *Piers* is clear, certainly as clear as the presence of problems concerning the Active and Contemplative lives; but that they constitute the central theme of the poem is doubtful. It seems unnecessary to hark back to a tradition nearly extinct, as Bloomfield admits,[27] well before Langland's time in order to account for these. Nor does it seem necessary to speculate about the existence and nature of an apocalyptic literary form to account for the literary nature of Langland's poem.[28] Bloomfield's argument is based on the assumption that spiritual writers who stressed social regeneration

---

[24] See also Bloomfield's "*Piers Plowman* and the Three Grades of Chastity", *Anglia*, LXXVI 1958), p. 227; and "*Piers Plowman* as a Fourteenth-Century Apocalypse", *The Centennial Review*, V (1961), pp. 281-95.
[25] *Piers Plowman as a Fourteenth-Century Apocalypse*, p. 105.
[26] *Ibid.*, "Preface", p. viii.
[27] *Ibid.*, pp. 45, 68.
[28] *Ibid.*, ch. I.

are a distinct group from those who stressed individual perfection, a distinction which he inconsistently admits is impossible to make.[29] He even seems to assume that true mystics, those belonging to the latter group, did not criticize society and urge reform. But the "prophets and prophetesses" Jusserand names are clear examples of mystical reformers, and one need only read the works of St. Bernard, who is sometimes called the "Father of Mysticism", whose personal career embraced both public and private pursuits, and who so dominated medieval spirituality as to be Dante's proper guide through the consummating experiences of Paradise,[30] to find the milieu in which Langland thought and wrote. In fact, one need only consider the *Divine Comedy* itself with its many literary resemblances to *Piers Plowman*. Similarly, Bloomfield's interpretations of several passages in *Piers* seem forced for the sake of his thesis. His considering Lady Church's explanation of salvation (B: Passus I) as having to do essentially with one's social obligations is a case in point.[31] I shall spend considerable time on this passage in order to show that while she is dealing with perfection rather than the ordinary state of grace, Lady Church's principal subject is individual rather than social perfection.

At any rate, final evaluation of Bloomfield's argument must await future scholarly developments; for now it is important to note that interest in Langland's concern with problems of spirituality spans the whole range of "modern" scholarship, growing more intense in more recent studies. Bloomfield's study is the first full-length discussion devoted exclusively to this aspect of *Piers*; at the same time, insofar as it concentrates on Langland's reformist zeal and associates him with writers concerned with perfection rather than ordinary salvation, Bloomfield's study also refers us back to Jusserand, with whom this "tradition" begins. Yet this relatively old approach has not unfolded the core of *Piers Plowman*, has not revealed the unifying thread of development in the poem. Even Bloomfield's interpretation, I feel, must take its

29   *Ibid.,* pp. 99-100.
30   *Paradiso,* XXXI-XXXIII.
31   *Ibid.,* pp. 152-53. See also pp. 105-107, and all of ch. V.

place beside other interpretations as bringing out a theme or aspect of Langland's work rather than its central concern.

What is called for now is serious consideration of Langland as a mystical writer: strict application to *Piers Plowman* of spirituality strictly taken. To view *Piers Plowman* as fundamentally concerned with individual perfection in the Unitive Life rather than with the broad catch-all problem of salvation is to find the possibility of comprehending, and giving perspective to, most of the themes and aspects already studied. By its very nature as both a branch of theology and a strategy for Christian living, spirituality proceeds from dogma, morals, psychology, and the personal experience of spiritual men and women. Such theological and moral problems as *temporalia*, learning, divine helps, and so on, are of especial importance to a soul seeking perfection, and practical concerns are fundamental in a quest that is largely a matter of ascetic effort. The personal and inward character of Langland's teaching, furthermore, reminds us of one of the few traits fourteenth-century mystics have in common. As Dom David Knowles has pointed out, it arises from the climate of the age:

the religious climate of the age was sympathetic to a personal and "mystical" approach to the way of perfection; the older conception of the monastic life as the only secure way of salvation, the ark in the flood, had lost its wide appeal and its place had been taken, for earnest seekers, by the way of personal, if not solitary, endeavour. Similarly, with the breakdown of the vast theological synthesis, the way of truth might be shown in a more concrete form by the seer – a Catherine of Sweden, a Bridget of Sweden or a Julian of Norwich – or found himself by the solitary contemplative.[32]

The mystical process, an inward, psychological process controlled by adherence to doctrines of faith, also offers an approach to the interpretation of both *Visio* and *Vita* that is consistent, and that may elucidate the organic relationships between these

---

[32] *Op. cit.,* p. 43. The first three chapters of Knowles's book, a sequel to his earlier *English Mystics* (New York, 1927), give a brief but excellent discussion of the nature and history of mysticism. For a discussion of the nature, sources, and methods of spirituality, see Reginald Garrigou-Lagrange, *Christian Perfection and Contemplation,* trans. by Sr. M. T. Doyle, O. P. (St. Louis, 1951), pp. 12-47.

and smaller parts of *Piers Plowman*. Few scholars have adhered
to a single avenue of approach in their analyses of the poem;
most interpret some parts as dealing with problems of the exterior
world, others, with problems of the interior life. R. W. Frank, Jr.,
for example, is typical in taking the *Visio* as concerned with man
in society, but the *Vita* as concerned with the spiritual needs of
the individual soul.[33] The general confusion is amply illustrated by
an argument presented by Donaldson:

> the *Vita* handles two basically different concepts at the same time
> and sometimes in the same terms. The chief difference between the
> concepts is that the first, as applied to the life of the individual, seems
> to develop in a sequence from outwardness (the active life) to in-
> wardness (the contemplative life) to inward-outwardness (the mixed
> life), while the second develops in a sequence of three stages of in-
> wardness, all of which, of course, have also appropriate outward
> manifestations and all of which are, incidentally, open to men of all
> vocations.[34]

Similarly, no scholar has justly acknowledged the degree of unity
that seems to inform the poem. Father Dunning and David
Fowler consider the A-text as comprising two separate works, gen-
erically related but independent.[35] Frank claims unity in the B-
version, but a serial unity rather than an organic one. With all
scholars he holds the theme of the whole poem to be the way
to salvation. This general theme he divides into three sub-themes:
the first vision of the *Visio* dramatizes the way to damnation, the
second, the way to salvation, the whole *Vita*, the necessity of good
works.[36] But since an adequate rationale of this tripartite division
of the general theme is not offered, the poem in Frank's interpretation remains a rather loose structure.

In this study, then, I seek to develop the approach to *Piers*
that seems promising, yet the possibilities of which have remained
unexplored. My most general objective is to show that Langland
fully belongs among the spiritual writers of the Middle Ages, and

[33] *Op. cit., passim.*
[34] *Op. cit.,* p. 159.
[35] Dunning, *Interpretation of the A-Text,* pp. 4-5, 167-69; Fowler, *op.
cit.,* pp. 4-7.
[36] *Op. cit.,* pp. 19-33.

that his poem must be read in the context of medieval mysticism properly understood. More specifically, I seek to argue that the poem's central and unifying concern is the soul's striving, not for the ordinary state of grace absolutely required for salvation, but for perfection,[37] a spiritual state involving such high degrees of sanctifying grace as bring the soul to mystical contemplation and the Unitive Life, thus to its surest hope of salvation. More particularly still, and since *Piers Plowman* is a poem and not a spiritual treatise, I wish to establish that the soul's progress through the mystical way is dramatized allegorically rather than developed discursively, and that its progress toward this goal is dramatized from the very beginning rather than only in the poem's later stages.

My argument consists of a detailed analysis of several key passages taken in themselves and in light of appropriate concepts from medieval spirituality. The two most important passages are those in which the way of salvation is forthrightly and fully explained, and that occur early in the poem where the movement toward the goal of salvation is initiated: that is, where the governing ideas of the entire work are laid out. The first of these is the conversation between Will and Lady Church in which Will asks how he may save his soul and Lady Church gives him a full, though compendious, answer. The second is Piers's description of the Highway to Truth, which is also a detailed explanation of the way of salvation, and which initiates a new beginning, a renewal of the soul's effort and progress. A careful study of

---

[37] I use the term *perfection,* both here and throughout this study, to signify relative perfection, the only kind possible on earth, as opposed to absolute perfection, possible only in heaven. Since perfection in this life is relative to that in the next, it is inexhaustible. To achieve perfection on earth means to achieve such spiritual excellence that the individual may be called perfect, but not a spiritual state beyond which there is no further growth. Quite the contrary, if one assumes he need pursue perfection no further, he is by that very act imperfect. "No one is perfect", St. Bernard says, "who does not wish to be still more perfect; the more perfect a man is, the more he reaches out to an even higher perfection". (Letter 35: to the Monk Drogo, in *The Letters of St. Bernard of Clairvaux,* trans. by Bruno Scott James, Chicago, 1953, pp. 68-69.) This is the very note on which *Piers Plowman* ends.

these passages reveals that the goal set before the individual is the mystic's goal, and the means are those of perfection. Later passages, particularly the end of *Dobet* and the beginning of *Dobest*, are analyzed less thoroughly, but sufficiently to suggest that at this point perfection is actually achieved. I do not intend, I wish to make clear, to offer a complete and systematic interpretation of *Piers Plowman*. Many intriguing scenes, Pier's Pardon in the *Visio*, for example, or the Banquet with the Doctor of Divinity in the *Vita,* remain hardly touched. I wish only to bring out the central and unifying element in the poem, thereby to provide a perspective that may lead to a full and satisfying interpretation.

In order that this study may lead to solutions of problems other than the poem's meaning, I concentrate on the relatively neglected C-text rather than the A or B.[38] In this way it is possible to note in all three texts the substantial identity in thought, and frequently the near identity in wording, of the crucial passages in which the quest for perfection is first undertaken and then fulfilled. Many large changes come into view as we move from A to B to C, but only minor changes in those passages that lay out the governing principles of the poem and that show those principles brought to fruition. And where there are changes, the C-version usually contains the clearest, most amplified, and most precise statements of the three. By concentrating on the C-text, then, and by noting and taking into account differences in the important passages, I hope to show that the quest for perfection governs all three versions from beginning to end, thus supporting the arguments that the *Visio* and *Vita* are a single poem even in the A-text, that one man, whom I call Langland, wrote all three versions, and that the C-version is Langland's most complete and definitive statement. For my part, predominant attention to the A and B-texts has contributed to failure to

[38] All quotations, unless otherwise indicated, are from Skeat's edition of the C-text (*The Vision of William Concerning Piers the Plowman in Three Parallel Texts Together With Richard the Redeless,* London, 1924, 2 vols.). Quotations of the B-text also come from Skeat, but quotations of A come from George Kane, *Will's Visions of Piers Plowman and Do-Well* (London, 1960).

understand this poem because it involves undue attention to passages, such as Piers's dramatic tearing of the pardon, that are misleading or even mistakenly included. The C-version, as Donaldson has convincingly argued, is the most perfect. I believe it should be taken as a standard for determining the details of meaning in the other two. I do not solve these problems in this study, of course, but I keep them in mind along the way and come to them directly, albeit not conclusively, at the end.

Pursuit of Langland's meaning, finally, leads one into study of many spiritual writers. One cannot avoid Thomas Aquinas, for example, as the authority for at least the commonplaces of medieval moral and spiritual concepts. His works are cited frequently in this study. Bernard of Clairvaux and Walter Hilton are cited most frequently, however, because they represent the preceding and the contemporary, the parent and the heir, the Continental and the English. Taken together, they provide a convenient enclosure for the spiritual tradition that has proven relevant to *Piers Plowman*.

II. THE DREAMER AS THE CENTER OF THE DRAMATIC ALLEGORY

The unity of *Piers Plowman* does not arise from the poem's discussion of either particular theological problems or specific social conditions, for there is no inherent continuity in these. Nor does it arise from the series of "settings", which supplant one another according to a very loose and vague imaginative logic in the *Visio*, and no logic at all in the *Vita*. The sequence of these materials depends for its continuity on something else: namely, the character of the Dreamer. Will's presence alone holds this poem together. The quest for salvation is his personal quest, or rather that of the individual soul, whom Will represents. The series of imaginative "settings" serves to externalize and dramatize the interior changes in Will, and what is discussed in successive visions arises from the problems Will faces in each stage of his spiritual transmutation. *Piers Plowman*, in other words, is governed by progress in the spiritual life, which "by definition", Father Dunning has reminded us, "is the *inner* life of the individual".[1]

Langland's primary aim, therefore, is not to discuss the way of salvation, but to dramatize the experiental undertaking of the way. I do not believe, as does Frank, that each vision comprises a thematic unit.[2] Rather the individual dream visions mark off stages in Will's development. Nor do I agree with Frank when he says: "All that is allegorical about [the poem] is the treatment of abstractions as though they were concrete."[3] The poem

---

[1] "Structure of the B-Text", p. 232.
[2] *Op. cit.*, p. 3.
[3] *Ibid.*, p. 2. See also Frank's "The Art of Reading Medieval Personification-Allegory", *ELH*, XX (1953), 237-50.

certainly uses personifications whose names are to be taken literally, but it also uses symbols, and the actions of both symbols and personifications take place in an allegorical context. What Frank omits to consider is the arena in which the events of the poem take place. After Will has undergone the initial act of conversion, the "real" setting of the poem, beginning with the Mede episode, is the interior man acting with his own faculties and reacting to forces from within and from the natural and supernatural worlds without. In parts of the *Vita,* especially in *Dowel,* where Will meets Thought, Wit, Study, Scripture, and other similar personifications, the personal and inward character of the poem is more apparent than it is in the *Visio* and in other parts of the *Vita* (the banquet with the Doctor of Divinity, for example, and most of *Dobest*). But the interior man is also the subject of the *Visio,* where the king's court, the church, the half-acre, and so on, are allegorical vehicles used to dramatize the condition of the soul and the changes that take place in it.

Langland's literary technique changes frequently: sometimes he uses his satirical targets as allegorical vehicles; sometimes he expresses his social views directly, using a more literary vehicle, such as the search for the dwelling of Dowel, to carry his allegory; sometimes he intermixes the allegorical and non-allegorical, as in the last part of *Dobet.* Here the Four Daughters have an allegorical meaning, but the vision of Christ is literally a vision of Christ. What never changes is the subject of the poem: growth in the spiritual life. In this respect the poem has an organic unity and a coherent development.

The opening of *Piers Plowman* lends validity to these observations. Of first importance to Will, and consequently to us, is that Will falls asleep and continues to awaken and fall asleep throughout the poem. Langland does not simply adopt this literary device as convenient and conventional, for at one point in the *Vita* of both B and C (the A-version breaks off long before) he indicates how his falling asleep is to be interpreted:

> 'slepynge, ich hadde grace
> To wite what Dowel ys . ac wakynge neuere!'
>
> (XIV:218-19) [4]

If Will did not fall asleep again, he would not go beyond this point; if he did not fall asleep at the beginning of the poem, nothing at all would have happened to him. Insofar as Will represents every individual, every individual must in some sense fall asleep if he is to undergo such change as will conduce to his salvation. For in the poet's view, to fall asleep means to receive the grace which makes knowledge, and thus growth, possible. Such a grace, of course, would be prevenient grace, by which the soul is called to desire to perform, and given the power to perform, each divine act in a definite series.[5] And since this grace prevenes the acquisition of knowledge, the knowledge gained is of truths that surpass man's natural powers. According to St. Thomas, God by his grace may sometimes miraculously instruct men in what can be known by natural reason;[6] but Will is not seeking divinely inspired natural knowledge, at least by the time he makes the above statement, because he says, emphatically and flatly, that he can *never* know Dowel while awake. Will is after truths that surpass man's natural knowledge, and that, again according to St. Thomas, absolutely require grace to be known.[7] This is the kind of truth, and the only kind, that leads man in this life to a knowledge of Truth itself. Will's falling asleep is directly related to his quest for Truth, and it has an allegorical significance. On Malvern Hills he receives the prevenient grace that initiates his movement toward salvation. Falling asleep again and again, he dramatizes one's need for

---

[4] The parallel line in the B-text does not mention grace, but it makes essentially the same point as the line in C: "wo was me thanne/That I in meteles ne myȝte . more haue yknowen" (XI:396-97). This is an instance of what I feel is true of the C-version generally: that far from being a different poem written by a different man, C perfects both A and B by adding clarifying detail, re-arranging material for the sake of order, amplitude, and balance, and making other changes that enhance the precision of thought.

[5] *Sum. Theo.,* I-II, q. 111, a. 3.

[6] *Ibid.,* q. 109, a. 1.

[7] *Ibid.*

ever more and more grace as one moves through an undertaking that grows increasingly difficult with each stage.[8] Each time he awakens he does not lose the grace already received, nor is his previous growth cancelled. On the contrary, while his eyes are open he remembers, wonders about, analyzes, and reasons from what he saw with his eyes closed; moreover, personifications continue to appear to him. But he does not continue his spiritual growth until he again falls asleep.

Knowledge is one of the particular effects of grace.[9] Its fundamental effect is to endow man with a spiritual life whereby all his natural powers may operate on a supernatural plane.[10] As man's natural life, which he has in respect of his sensitive and corporeal nature, places him in the society of other corporeal beings, so his spiritual life, which he has in respect of his mind, places him in the society of spiritual beings, of God and the angels.[11] The effect of Will's falling asleep for the first time is that his attention is immediately transferred from the world of the natural life to that of the spiritual life. The world of the soft May sun, the slumbrous land, and (in the B-text) the hypnotic stream gives way momentarily to the world in which the Tower, Field, and Dale are neighboring dwelling places separated by geographical metaphors only, and not at all by the total division that exists between the temporal, material order and the eternal, spiritual order. It is all one country, all one order of time, and all one plane of reality. The field remains a natural world in itself, but is not simply the world of the natural life; its elements are now involved in man's relation to God (II: 17-19). The food, drink, and clothing it provides have a spiritual importance rather than a biological, economic, or social importance merely (II:20-

---

[8]   Here again I disagree with Frank who says that the use of individual visions as thematic units is "the only reasonable explanation for this plurality of dreams" (*op. cit.*, p. 3). I do agree however, with Elizabeth Salter's view of the signifiance of dreams in Langland (*op. cit.*, pp. 58-62). My discussion of dreams may serve to complement hers.

[9]   See *Sum. Theo.*, I-II, q. 109, a. 1.

[10]   See *Sum. Theo.*, I-II, q. 110, a. 1, obj. 2 and rep. obj. 2; a. 2, rep. obj. 1 and rep. obj. 2; also q. 112, a. 1.

[11]   See Étienne Gilson, *Théologie et Histoire de la Spiritualité* (Paris, 1943), pp. 11-12. Also *Sum. Theo.*, II-II, q. 23, a. 1, rep. obj. 1.

32); "the moneye of this molde" (II: 41-53), dismissed in its purely economic significance by the *"Reddite Cesari"* text, is important only insofar as it affects the life of the spirit. Thus the world of *Piers Plowman* is established at the outset as the world of the spiritual life, one in which an angel may come down to speak to the commune (B-text), or Conscience may address the king (C-text), and Lady Church may descend from the Tower to speak to Will.

The drama of the poem begins when Will's consciousness is transferred by his first sleep into the world of the spiritual life.[12] He immediately undergoes changes by which his own spirit enters into life: that is, his mind is enlightened and his affections are stirred until, falling on his knees before Lady Church, he makes the initial act of conversion. "Our true life is found only through conversion", St. Bernard says,

nor is there any other entrance into life, as the Lord says again: *Unless you be converted and become as little children, you shall not enter into the kingdom of heaven* (Matt. xviii, 3).[13]

The initial infusion of grace has spiritualized his awareness and ennobled his understanding. Whereas awake he attended only to "cellis . and selcouthe thynges" (I:5), asleep he is aware of the world as situated between the habitations of Truth on the one side, and death and the wicked spirits on the other (I:14-21). He is called, in other words, from a sense awareness of things in the world to a transcendent, spiritual awareness of human life. He perceives further that the Field is crowded with persons engaged in various activities, some morally praiseworthy, most blameworthy. And his attention is not limited to an observation of externals; it concentrates on the inward lives of the people – how they are motivated by habits of virtue or vice, and how the ecclesiastics among them, supposedly of superior moral education,

---

[12] Since the progress of *Piers* is essentially dramatic, centering on the change of thought and feeling in Will, and since Will's development begins immediately upon his first falling asleep, the change in title of the first section from *Prologus* in A and B to *Passus I* in C is a proper one.
[13] *Of Conversion*, trans. by Watkin Williams (London, 1938), p. 1. This translation will be used throughout.

contradict a right conscience.[14] He then becomes aware of
the principle of organization of a large part of the Field,[15] seeing
it not as it is, but as it ought to be. Social life in the Field should
be ordered according to a hierarchy of mutually serving classes,
and the law under which society is governed should be admin-
istered in light of its coming through the king from Christ and
having as its aim the salvation of the entire commune.[16] Again
he perceives more than the material constitution of the commune,
but the immaterial sources as well, Conscience and Kynde Wit,
which reveals that although the commune has a divine sanction
and an ultimately divine law, it also springs from a natural, inward, human necessity. He further sees that the order of the
commune must be maintained even though its head seems an
intolerable tyrant.[17] In this way Will comes to understand the
Field in its several parts and principles very well, so well that
Lady Church does not touch on the Establishing of the Commune and Fable of the Rats at all, and she dwells on the folk
in general only long enough to reduce the moral problems they
raise to the single, ultimate problem of their worshipping the
goods of this world rather than those of heaven (II:5-9).

What Will is not able to see directly, but learns through *doctrina* under the tutelage of Lady Church, is what the Tower and
Dale have to do with the Field. The Lady explains, in summary,
that according to God's wish and creative design, the goods of
the Field are but the instruments by which, and the material
conditions under which, man is to find his ultimate happiness
in God (II:12-33); that measure is the objective rule of action by
which worldly goods are made instrumental to man's salvation
(*Ibid.*); that the life of the soul has priority and authority over

[14]   In the C-text, I:95-138. Conscience does not appear in A or B, but his
appearance in C is consistent with the level of perception manifested in
both earlier versions.
[15]   The commune is not coextensive with the Field, which represents the
world in general rather than society in particular. Thus Langland includes
in the Field persons who do not participate in any of the classes that
form the commune: the anchoresses and hermits, who live a solitary life
(I:27-32).
[16]   The Establishing of the Commune (I:139-57).
[17]   The Fable of the Rats (I:165-217).

the life of the body (II:34-40); that money also comes under the rule of measure (II:41-55); and that the Devil's design, pursued by falsifying the true nature of worldly goods in order that man may take these proximate means as his ultimate end, is to lead man to an everlasting existence in the Dale (II:55-67). Will understands all of this discussion perfectly; he objects to none of it. On the contrary, the impact of these insights brings about the beginning of his conversion, one of feeling as well as mind:

> Thanne knelede ich on my knees . and criede hure of grace,
> And preiede hure pytously . to preie for me to amende,
> Al-so to kenne me kyndlich . on crist to by-leue,
> 'And teche me to no tresour . bote telle me thys ilke,
> How ich may sauy my saule . that seynt art yholde.'
>
> (II:76-80)

In this act culminate the changes Will has undergone from the very beginning of the poem.

At the point where Will desires conversion, the true subject of the poem emerges; and until this point it does not emerge. What Will sees in passus 1 prepares him for the teaching of Lady Church, and what he learns from her in the first part of passus 2 awakens in him the realization that the soul is a saintly thing, and moves him to desire to amend, learn to live in Christ, and know the means of saving his soul. The issues brought up before Will's question, therefore, are not themselves the essential subject of the poem, but are pedagogically and inspirationally instrumental in evoking from Will a response that, expressed, indicates to the reader the subject with which Langland is dealing.

Now Will does not ask how society is to be reformed. Passus 1 makes it clear that he already has solutions to this problem. He knows that the activities of the folk in the Field are caused interiorly by virtuous or vicious motives; he knows that the corrupt practices of the friar-preachers, who make charity an occasion for commerce, can be stopped by the Church; he knows that the pardoners can be put out of business by the bishop if the bishop would respond to what he hears; he has heard Conscience tell the commune about the evils of absenteeism; and in the Establishing of the Commune and the Fable of the Rats, he has seen by what principles a society ought to live in order to preserve its goodness. Nor does Will ask what is the proper use of worldly goods. This question has already been answered in the preliminary discussion; it is part of the context out of which the real issue of the poem comes, rather than the issue itself. And Will has understood this answer. Indeed, he is not interested in worldly goods, for he asks Lady Church to direct him to no treasure but the thing itself.[18]

Will asks, instead, how he personally may save his soul, and insofar as Will speaks for every man, he asks how any individual may achieve salvation. Lady Church's answer, that one must become a true man on earth through growth in love, is a fundamental answer applicable to each individual, whether he lives in society as king, commoner, cleric, or peasant, or lives the solitary life of the "ancres and eremites . that holden hem in hure cellys" (I:30). Will's personal salvation, furthermore, is not affected by either the existence or the removal of political and economic corruption. Indeed, the concrete circumstances we are given about Will's personal life place him outside the society that is satirized: he belongs to none of the classes of society by vocation, and far from being guilty himself of the social evils he sees, his readiness to condemn them has frequently to be restrained. The subject of *Piers Plowman*, the *Visio* included, is not man in society, or the reform of society that cannot be brought about unless each individual reforms; it is personal salvation purely and simply. Langland is certainly interested in reg-

---

[18]   I am alluding specifically, of course, both to Bloomfield's interpretation and to Father Dunning's interpretation of the A-*Visio*. Dunning, I feel, relies too much on the preliminary issues raised by Lady Church rather than on the central issue. He takes the *Reddite Cesari* text as equal in importance to *Deus caritas,* even though the former governs only 15 lines in the Skeat edition Dunning uses, while the latter governs 124. The question of money is included more for the sake of completeness (as what is left besides food, drink, and clothing) than as a matter of central concern. That the A-text does not include the Establishing of the Commune and the Fable of the Rats does not qualify my argument. The absence of these does not change the meaning of what is expressed in A, Lady Church's discussion is substantially identical in all three versions, and the manner in which the central issue emerges out of Will's experience is essentially the same in A as in B and C.

istering social complaint and uses his poem as an occasion for expressing his views; but these matters are incorporated into the poem, they are not the issue that governs its development. The "true poem" is governed by what the medieval world saw as the universal, timeless, spiritual, and personal question of what a man ought to become in this life in view of God's being his true destiny, and how he may reach this goal.

The subject of *Piers Plowman*, then, is directly tied to Will as the focal point of consciousness in the poem and as the representative of each individual soul. It is expressed by Will himself, arises out of the internal change he undergoes in the first part of the poem, and is a problem that concerns him personally. If we understand the essential nature of conversion we see that the entire *Visio*, where Will is not constantly before our eyes, as well as the *Vita*, where his presence is constant, develops dramatically the internal changes that take place in him.

St. Bernard provides a description of what happens when one is converted. He describes this phenomenon as a psychological change initiated by the voice of God:

conversion of souls is the work of the Divine, not of the human voice. Simon, son of John (*John* xxi, 15), called and appointed by the Lord to be a fisher of men, even he will toil all night in vain and take nothing, until casting the net at the Lord's word he encloses a great multitude of fishes.[19]

God speaks, furthermore, inwardly in the soul[20] and opens the ears of the soul whether the soul wills to listen or not:

Truly it needs not that we labour to hear this voice; rather were it a labour so to close thine ears as not to hear it. Indeed it offers itself; it imposes itself; never does it cease to knock at the door of each one of us.[21]

God's word, finally, a word of both light and power, not only enlightens the soul but also moves it to a scrutiny of itself: it brings the soul face to face with itself:

[19] *Of Conversion,* p. 2.
[20] *Ibid.,* p. 3.
[21] *Ibid.,* p. 4.

Return, ye transgressors, to the heart (Isa. xlvi, 8). Now this is what the Lord said to begin with, and this word addressed to all these who are being converted in heart seems to have come first, a word which not merely calls them back, but leads them back and sets them before their own faces.[22]

Under the metaphor of the voice of God, St. Bernard is speaking principally of grace, but specifically of a grace that, working within the soul, prevenes knowledge, and such knowledge as causes an affective change that moves the soul to examine itself. Conversion comes about through self-knowledge, and through no other way:

Apply thy hearing within, use the eyes of thy heart, and by thine own testing thou wilt learn its state. For no one knows what is in man, except the spirit of man which is in him (I Cor. ii, 11).[23]

Will's experience in the first two passus is similar to that described by St. Bernard. Falling asleep, he is called; perceiving the human spiritual condition by direct sight first and then more deeply by instruction from Lady Church, he is not only called back, but led back. The voice of Conscience heard in passus 1 is already the voice of God speaking within. St. Bernard describes the conscience as one of the agents through which the voice of God is inwardly heard:

To go back, however, to the subject of that voice of which we spoke at first. It behoves us to return while the way still lies open by which he, who with such fatherly anxiety recalls those who have erred in heart, may show us his salvation. Nor let us meanwhile resent the gnawing of the worm within, nor let a perilous weakness of mind, a deadly softness, have power to persuade us to seek to hide our present discomfort. It is far better for the worm to be felt then, when it can be suffocated. Accordingly, let it gnaw now, so that it may die and, as it dies, little by little cease to gnaw.[24]

[22] *Ibid.,* p. 4.
[23] *Ibid.,* p. 6.
[24] *Ibid.,* p. 11. The passage I quote is the first statement of chapter V. That Bernard is speaking of conscience here is indicated by the heading of this chapter: *That the reproach of an accusing conscience should be both felt and removed in this present life, lest it abide with us in eternity.* Incidentally, the addition of Conscience's appearance in C (I:95-138) is another instance in which the C-version perfects the earlier versions by

The voice of Lady Church is a more profound and more direct voice from God, for she comes down from God's dwelling to speak to Will. She speaks as *Magistra*, drawing from the *Magisterium*, which includes not only revelation as guarded and officially interpreted by the Church, but also the common teaching of theologians. This is the aspect of Lady Church that overawes Will:

> Thanne hadde ich wonder in my wit . what womman hue were,
> That suche wyse wordes . of holy wryt shewede;
> And halsede hure on the heie name . er hue thennys wente,
> What hue were witterly . that wissede me so and tauhte.
>
> (II:68-71)

After Will is called back and led back, he undergoes a change of heart and mind that, according to the process described by St. Bernard, sets him before his own face:

What then is the purpose of that ray of light, of that word, if not that the soul may know itself? Indeed the book of conscience is laid open, a wretched past is recalled, a sad story is unfolded. The reason is enlightened and the record of the memory is, as it were, submitted to its scrutiny. But both reason and memory are not so much possessions of the soul, as they are the soul itself; thus it is the soul which, at once both inspector and inspected, is set before its own face and compelled by the violent apparitors of thoughts which arise against it (*Rom*. ii, 15) to be judged in the first instance at its own bar.[25]

This self-confrontation begins with the Meed episode, at the point where Will asks to know the false (III:4). In the previous two passus Will was not personally involved in what he saw in the Field: that is, there was nothing of himself at stake in it.

---

making the progress of the poem more explicitly clear. The Angel (B-Pro: 128-38) for whom Conscience is substituted also represents the voice of God, but the Angel is "too supernatural" a being for Will to see at this stage in his progress. In a way the Angel is "more supernatural" than Lady Church. Will's visions begin on a level close to the natural and progress until, in the *Vita*, he sees not only Christ but the Holy Ghost. The increasingly supernatural character of the dream visions in the four large sections of the poem (*Visio, Dowel, Dobet,* and *Dobest*) is one of its unifying principles, and arises from the increasingly spiritualized awareness developing in Will.

25   *Ibid.*, p. 5.

Rather he observed the actions of the folk and expressed his praise or condemnation from a distance. Now, however, what he sees concerns him personally, for desirous of salvation he asked to be shown this vision. As soon as Lady Church directs his attention to the vices, furthermore, Will makes an outgoing response to Lady Meed, revealing for the first time his moral vulnerability:

> Hure a-raye with hure rychesse . rauesshede myn herte.
>
> (III:16)

And just before she leaves him, Lady Church says:

> Know hym wel, yf thow kanst . and kep the fro hem alle
> That louyeth hure lordsheps . lasse other more.
> Lacke hem noȝt, bote lete hem worthe . tyl Leaute be iustice,
> And haue power for to punyshe hem . then put forth thy reson
> For ich by-kenne the Crist,' quath hue . 'and hus clene moder,
> Encombre neuere thy conscience . for couetyse of Mede,'
>
> (III:47-52)

indicating again that the vision of Meed is meant for Will's moral enlightment in order to bring about in him a moral change.

Thus Will, Everyman, becomes both inspector and inspected, seeing the corruption his soul is, and has been, capable of and how it is able to move out of its corruptibility. The passage from St. Bernard last quoted is already a capsule interpretation of Meed's attempted marriage with False, her debate with Conscience, and her final expulsion by the King: its reason enlightened and its memory scrutinized, the soul is "compelled by the violent apparitors of thoughts which arise against it to be judged in the first instance at its own bar". The words "apparitors" and "bar" evoke a scene similar to that in Langland, and Bernard's continuation of this point, in which he lists the kinds of vices the soul may find in its memory, suggests the kinds of vices depicted in and around Lady Meed:

If there be hidden within thee pride, or envy, or avarice, or ambition, or any such pest, scarcely will it be able to escape this scrutiny. If fornication, or rapine, or cruelty, or any kind of deceit, indeed, whatever fault you will, be there, it may not be hidden from the judge within who is himself the accused; nor in his presence will it be denied. For, however quickly passed all the prurience of sinful flesh, however soon ended all voluptuous charm, it impressed the thoughts of its bitterness upon the memory; it left its foul traces.[26]

The Meed episode, therefore, and, since it dramatizes but the first step toward full conversion, the entire *Visio*, has a double function. In one respect it exposes individual kinds and causes of corruption among the classes of society, in another it describes dramatically the state and progress of the interior man as he begins his personal conversion. Its double character is evident in Lady Church's last statement to Will (quoted above). As later instructors will do, Lady Church admonishes Will to:

> Lacke hem noȝt, bote lete hem worthe . tyle Leaute be iustice,
> And haue power for to punyshe hem . then put forth the reson,
> $\qquad$ (III:49-50)

thus indicating that social evils will be revealed for what they are, and that Will, who never could abide them, is not to take justice into his own hands and carry on a public campaign against them. At the same time, however, she advises Will to:

> Know hym wel, yf thow kanst . and kep the fro hem alle
>
> . $\quad$. $\quad$. $\quad$. $\quad$. $\quad$. $\quad$. $\quad$. $\quad$. $\quad$. $\quad$. $\quad$.
>
> Encombre neuere thy conscience . for couetyse of Mede,
> $\qquad$ (III:47, 52)

thus indicating that the public vices also signify private vices, for Will is not a king, or a counselor, or confessor, or a rich patron of a church, and thus cannot be corrupted by these vices as literally depicted. And if Will must not condemn these vices in their public manifestations, he must condemn them as they represent vices of the individual soul, for Lady Church's admonition that Will avoid them presupposes that he condemn them. Unless we understand this passage as having a two-fold reference, it makes no sense. In the same way must be understood all dramatizations of social conditions, wherever in the poem they appear.

[26] *Ibid.,* p. 6.

III. THE DREAMER'S DESIRE FOR PERFECTION

The most important fact about the subject of *Piers Plowman* has yet to be discussed: namely, that Langland dramatizes the way to perfection rather than simple salvation, and that the quest for perfection governs the *Visio* as well as the *Vita*. Such scholars as Henry W. Wells, Nevill Coghill, and R. W. Chambers, proponents of the three-lives interpretation, are aware that perfection is the concern of the later parts of the poem,[1] and Elizabeth Zeeman (Salter) argues briefly that perfection is the goal of Piers's Highway to Truth.[2] But the desire for perfection is expressed even earlier – when Will asks Lady Church how he may save his soul.

One cannot automatically assume, as many scholars seem to do, that by salvation Will means whatever one ordinarily means, especially because Will has in mind a state to be achieved in this life. This last point is made clear in Lady Church's answer:

"Whanne alle tresours ben tried,' quath hue . 'treuthe
   is the beste;
Ich do hit on *Deus caritas* . to deme the sothe.
Hit is as derworthe a druwery . as dere god him-selue.
For he, is trewe of hus tonge . and of hus two handes,
And doth the werkes therwith . and wilneth no man ille,

[1] H. W. Wells, "The Construction of *Piers Plowman*", *PMLA*, XLIV (1929), 123-40; "The Philosophy of *Piers Plowman*", *PMLA*, LIII (1938), 339-49. Nevill Coghill, "The Character of Piers Plowman Considered from the B-text", *Medium Aevum*, II (1933), 108-35; *The Pardon of Piers Plowman*, Sir Israel Gollancz Memorial Lecture, British Academy (London, 1945). R. W. Chambers, *Man's Unconquerable Mind* (London, 1939), pp. 88-171.
[2] "Piers Plowman and the Pilgrimage to Truth", *Essays and Studies*, XI (1958), 1-16.

He is a god by the gospel . and graunty may hele,
And like our Lorde also . by seynt Lukys wordes.

(II:81-87)

Since truth is as precious a possession as God himself, it is not
God himself; and since to be a true man is to work with true
hands and tongue and wish no man ill, such spiritual stature is
to be achieved on earth, where alone these problems exist. Con-
ceived as an earthly goal, salvation has as many forms as there
are forms of Christian life, and as many sets of means as there
are programs of Christian living. As Chaucer's Parson well knew,
"Manye been the weyes espirituels that leden folk to our Lord
Jhesu Crist, and to the regne of glorie." [3] Fundamentally, however, there are two spiritual goals a Christian may strive for in
this life in order to possess life in the next: (1) an ordinary state
of grace achieved by the common means that bring into the soul
the lower degrees of sanctifying grace; (2) a state of spiritual
sanctity achieved by the especially difficult means that merit
the higher degrees of sanctifying grace. The means of the former
goal involve faith in the articles of the Creed, reception of the
sacraments, obedience to the commandments, and so on. The
means of the latter goal include those of the former, but also
involve foregoing the goods of the world as far as possible, subduing the propensity to sin by mortification and penance, performance of unusually difficult good works, and meditation on and
contemplation of spiritual matters. [4] The latter goal, in other words,
is the goal of the mystic. In view of these two basic conceptions,
it is necessary, if we are to understand *Piers Plowman*, to determine how Langland conceives of the way to salvation at the
point where he raises the issue. Taken in its context, Will's

---

[3] *The Parson's Tale,* 1. 78, in F. N. Robinson, *The Works of Geoffrey
Chaucer,* 2nd edition (Boston, 1957), p. 229.
[4] Almost any recent discussion of spirituality supplies a full exposition of
these two Christian vocations – and also the theological controversies their
study has engendered. One of the best works covering the whole matter is
Garrigou-Lagrange, *op. cit.* This work is especially useful because it develops the medieval view of Christian perfection.

question opens the way to the mystic's goal rather than that of
the ordinary Christian.

Since the question of salvation comes out of Will's mouth and
expresses a personal desire, his knowledge of morality and his
conscious dedication to Christian ideals must be taken into account. The knowledge and faith he brings to the experience he
presently undergoes are already more than ordinary. Lady Church
reveals that Will is a baptized Christian who has promised to
believe in, be obedient to, and love the Church all his lifetime
(II:72-75). The C-text conversation with Reason and Conscience
on Cornhill, dramatizing Will's "romynge in remembraunce"
(VI:11), supplies more detailed information about his previous
education and spiritual commitment:

> 'Whanne ich ʒong was', quath ich . 'meny ʒer hennes.
> My fader and my frendes . founden me to scole,
> Tyle ich wiste wyterliche . what holy wryt menede,
> And what is best for the body . as the bok telleth,
> And sykerest for the soule . by so ich wolle continue.
>
> (VI:35-39)

Explaining that since he left school he has been singing "for
hure soules . of suche as me helpen" (VI:48), Will indicates that
he not only knows "holy wryt", "the bok", as mentioned above,
but also the "*paternoster* and my prymer . *placebo* and *dirige*,
/ And my sauter ... and my seuene psalmes" (VI:46-47). He
further explains that he is a tonsured ecclesiastic, an heir of
heaven, a minister of Christ, and one freed from the obligation
of manual labor by the Levitical Law (VI: 54-62).

His moral commentary on the folk in the field, spoken before
Lady Church descends for his instruction, also establishes Will
at the outset as being of relatively superior moral sensitivity. His
condemnation of wicked laymen is adamant, and his indigation
at the practice of various ecclesiastics is even more unyielding.
At several points he must restrain his critical temper. Viewing
the minstrels, to take one example from all three texts, and ready
to prove that St. Paul preached against them, he must check
himself with the reminder that "*Qui turpiloquium loguitor* . ys
Lucyfers knaue" (I:40). His judgments, furthermore, both favor-

able and unfavorable, rest specifically on the reality of future salvation and damnation. Thus the anchoresses and hermits are praised, on the one hand, because out of love of Christ and hope of heavenly bliss they apply themselves to prayers and penances rather than to seeking bodily satisfactions (1:27-32); while the absentee curates, on the other hand, are warned that God will take vengeance on them for their sins, and that Christ may curse them in the end for their lack of devotion (I:118-27). In short, Will enters the experience depicted in the poem with firm standards based on religious and moral truths, and with the ability and zeal to apply these standards to concrete situations. If Will had ordinary salvation in mind when he poses his question to Lady Church, he would be asking about what he already knows.

Nor is Will intellectually dull in seeming not to understand his instructors. It is never the case that he simply does not understand; it is always the case that he has no "kynde knowyng." The first instance of his use of this phrase comes after Lady Church has explained that no treasure is better than truth and true love (II:136):

> 'Ich haue no kynde knowyng,' quath ich . 'ʒe mote kenne me bettere,
> By what wey hit wexith . and wheder out of my menyng.'
>
> (II:137-38)

Will is not asking Lady Church to re-explain what she has already said in the previous 55 lines. He desires a solution to a more immediate and practical problem: how one actually grows in truth. He also desires to know whether such growth is "out of my menyng." Elsewhere Skeat glosses "menyng" as "intention" or "endeavor" (B, XV:467), but here as "intelligence" or "understanding", thereby reducing Will's statement to absurdity. Skeat would have Will ask to understand how love grows, and also to understand whether he cannot understand it. "Menyng" has the same significance here as it has elsewhere: Will seeks to know whether growth in love is beyond his endeavor.

"Kynde knowyng" must be understood in light of the practicality of Will's request. This phrase does not mean "natural understanding", as is sometimes maintained,[5] implying that Will is admitting small intellectual capacity, for Langland has a phrase to convey this meaning:

> For by lawe of *Levitici* . that our lord ordeynede,
> Clerkes that aren crouned . of kynde vnderstondyng
> Sholde nother swynke ne swete . ne swere at enquestes.
>
> VI:55-57)

Far from admitting a weak native intelligence, Will is here defending his refusal to engage in manual labor on the grounds of being one of those crowned with "kynde vnderstondyng". "Kynde knowying", on the other hand, means knowledge that is known immediately rather than mediately, that engages the affections as well as the intellect, and that is ultimately experiential. In his objection to Lady Church, quoted above, Will is saying that he has never experienced the truth she speaks of, and therefore she must teach him in a more practical way how it grows in the soul, and whether it is possible for him actually to become the true man she describes. The answer Lady Church makes to Will's request supports this defininition:

> Hit is a kynde knowyng . that kenneth in thyn herte
> For to louye thy lord . leuest of alle,
> And deye rathere than to do . any dedlich synne.
>
> (II:142-44)

'Kynde knowyng" is in the heart, affective as well as cognitive. Later in the same statement Lady Church repeats the phrase:

> Of kynde knowyng in herte . ther comseth a myghte,
> That falleth to the fader . that formede ous alle.
>
> (II:162-63)

Again, it is a heartfelt knowledge. To know love "kyndely" is

---

[5] David Fowler, for example, in *Piers Plowman: Literary Relations of the A and B Texts,* p. 20. R. W. Frank, Jr. translates this phrase as "natural knowledge" but does not explain its meaning, except to say it indicates "the inherent desire of the soul for the good". Frank also discusses the meanings Father Dunning and Greta Hort give to this phrase, rejecting both and making the valid point that "kynde knowyng" and "kynde wit" are not synonymous (*Piers Plowman and the Scheme of Salvation,* p. 47, n. 1).

really to have it in one's heart – to be loving – thus to feel a power that is the power of the Creator communicated to man. This power, of course, is the Holy Spirit, Charity itself, who sheds love abroad in the heart. To know love "kyndely" is to be consciously aware of the Holy Spirit dwelling in one's heart.

Will is a practical Christian. *Doctrina* satisfies him only when it is power as well as light, when it is efficacious in producing a real change. He fullfills St. Bernard's reminder that the individual must strive not merely to know, but to comprehend:

We should endeavour "to comprehend with all the saints what is the breadth, and length, and height, and depth" (Ephes. iii. 18). Notice how he tells us not simply *to know* but to *comprehend*, so that we should not rest content with the knowledge which gratifies curiosity, but should strive with all diligence to render our knowledge fruitful. The fruit of knowledge consists in the comprehension of its object, not in the mere knowing. For "to him who knoweth to do good and doth it not, that is, comprehends not the good he knoweth, to him it is sin" (James iv. 17). And St. Paul himself says in another place, "So run that you may comprehend" (I Cor. ix. 24).[6]

Rather than to know about God, Will seeks to know God in some immediate way. He seeks wisdom rather than knowledge, the gift of the Holy Ghost, which, perfecting charity, is a quasi-experiental knowledge of God directing the soul to contemplation of divine things and to judgment of all things according to divine rules.[7] In Walter Hilton's terms, Will seeks reform in both faith and feeling, which is the aim of those seeking perfection:

the first, reform in faith only, is sufficient for salvation; the second merits a great reward in the happiness of heaven ... The first kind of reform belongs only to beginners and those who are making progress in the spiritual life, and to men leading the active life. The second is for the perfect and contemplatives. By the first reform the image of sin is not destroyed and remains capable of making itself felt. But the second reform takes away the consciousness of this image of sin, and by the power of the Holy Ghost makes the soul aware of the workings of grace in it.[8]

[6]   *On Consideration*, V, xiii, trans. by a Priest of Mount Melleray (Dublin, 1921), p. 192.
[7]   *Sum. Theo.*, II-II, q. 45, a. 1, 3.
[8]   *The Scale of Perfection*, modernized by Dom Gerard Sitwell, O.S.B. (London, 1953), II, 5, pp. 153-54.

Until he begins to move toward a conscious awareness of the life of grace, until he begins to see in his heart the "myghte, / That falleth to the fader" (II:162-63), Will continues to seek a "kynde knowyng". After *Liberum Arbitrium* responds to Will's request that he "telle and teche me . to Charite" (XIX:2) by placing in his view *Cor-hominis* itself with *Ymago-dei* growing exactly in the center ("Euene in the myddes", XIX:6); after *Liberum Arbitrium* thus initiates a series of visions which culminate with Will's actually seeing the Passion of Christ, the Harrowing of Hell (Passus XXI), and the descent of *Spiritus Paraclitus* (Passus XXII), who "is Cristes messager, / And cometh fro the grete god . Grace is hus name" (XXII:207-08) – after Will begins this phase of his development, he no longer protests that he has no "kynde knowyng".[9]

Piers Plowman dwells at length, and throughout, on the practices of those engaged in the active life, and Will is aware of evils found in all states of life and is anxious to expose them. But he himself is an *actif* in a small degree circumstantially, not at all temperamentally. Will is a contemplative man, although he apparently does not, and need not, belong to a comtemplative order. His being married places him in the active life officially, but only insofar as he must provide for his wife and daughter as well as himself does he pursue this life. That he is not a member of any of the social classes, or guilty of the social evils depicted here, has already been discussed. We have also seen, in the C-text conversation with Reason and Conscience on Cornhill, that his life is a life of prayer rather than manual labor. By prayer he sustains himself and his family, and seems content to earn by this means only what is absolutely essential for life. Indeed, he seems to circulate among lollers and hermits, and, again because of his moral sensitivity, not very amicably:

---

[9]   R. W. Frank, Jr., *op. cit.,* pp. 47-48, has noted that Will's requests for a "kynde knowyng" cease after the appearance of *Liberum Arbitrium* (Soul in the B-text) and concludes that with the explanation of charity, Will's quest for a knowledge of goodness is ended. Actually, Will is just beginning to know love "kyndely".

> Thus ich a-waked, god wot . whanne ich wonede on
>   Cornehull,
> Kytte and ich in a cote . clothed as a lollere,
> And lytel y-lete by . leyue me for sothe,
> Among lollares of London. and lewede heremytes;
> For ich made of tho men . as reson me tauhte.

(VI:1-5)

Working in the world only so far as is necessary, but walking in it, scrutinizing it, and judging it, Will is neither envious nor covetous of the comforts enjoyed by other men.[10] Knowledge alone arouses his possessiveness, and arouses it to a fault. To *Liberum Arbitrium*, the last instructor to berate him for his curiosity, Will says:

> '3e, syre,' ich seyde, 'by so . that no man were
>   a-greued,
> All the science vnder sonne . and alle sotile craftes
> Ich wolde ich knewe and couthe . kyndeliche in myn
>   herte.'

(XVII:209-11)

Here is the last instance in which Will expresses a desire to know "kyndeliche" (and the added phrase, "in myn herte", defines this kind of knowledge). But the rebuke he thereupon receives is not for how he wishes to know, but for the scope of his desire to know (XVII:212-371). Why his curiosity is a fault is made clear in the first statement of *Liberum Arbitrium's* rebuke:

> 'Thanne art thow inparfyt,' quath he ...   (XVII:212)

By the standards of ordinary morality the folk of the world are judged; but Will himself is judged by the standards of perfection.

For such a person there can be no goal but perfection. If we turn again to the remainder of Will's conversation with Reason and Conscience on Cornhill, we find that perfection is, indeed, his goal:

> For-thy rebuke me ryght nought . Reson, ich 3ow praye;
> For in my conscience ich knowe . what Crist wolde that
>   ich wrouhte.

---

[10]   Although, as indicated by his spontaneous reaction to Lady Meed, he is not at the beginning of his conversion free of temptation.

Preyers of a parfyt man . and penaunce discret
Ys the leueste labour . that oure lord pleseth.
Non de solo,' ich seide . 'for sothe *uiuit homo,*
Nec in pane & pabulo . the *pater-noster* witnesseth;
Fiat voluntas tua . fynt ous alle thynges.'

(VI:82-88)

Prayer on behalf of those who help him, Will is aware, is not
enough; Christ wants the prayers of a perfect man, one whose
will is to do God's will (*Fiat voluntas tua*). Conscience takes
him at his word, again criticizing him according to the standard
of perfection. By associating perfection with taking a vow of
obedience to a religious superior, Conscience indicates the strict
sense in which the term *perfection* is to be taken:

"Quath Conscience, 'by Christ . ich can nat see this
    lyeth;
Ac it semeth nouht parfytnesse . in cytees for to begge,
Bote he be obediencer . to pryour other to mynstre.'

(VI:89-91)

And Will, finally, is not only aware of what perfection consists,
he hopes to achieve it in this life:

So hope ich to haue . of hym that is al-myghty
A gobet of hus grace . and bygynne a tyme,
That alle tymes of my tyme . to profit shal turne.'

(VI:99-101)

Which is to say that he hopes to achieve a spiritual state in which
his will so conforms to God's will that thenceforth every moment
of this life shall be meritorious for the next. Conscience and
Reason then advise Will not only to begin the life that leads to
perfection, but also to continue in that life until perfection is
actually achieved. Whereupon Will goes to church – not to
the field or to a manual task, but, again, to prayer – and prays
for a purpose different from that of the prayers he said for those
who gave him worldly sustenance:

'Ich rede the', quath Reson tho . rape the to
    by-gynne
The lyfe that ys lowable . and leel to the soule' –
'ȝe, and continue'; quath Conscience . and to the
    kirke ich wente.

> And to the kirke gan ich go . god to honourie,
> By-for the crois on my knees . knocked ich my brest,
> Sykinge for my synnes . seggynge my *pater-noster*,
> Wepyng and wailinge . tyle ich was a slepe.
>
> (VI:102-108)

Will's aim, therefore, is salvation through perfection rather than through an ordinary state of grace. By expressing his aim in terms of prayer, and by saying specifically the *pater-noster* as he again takes up the way, Will indicates both the point he has reached as the result of the changes dramatized in the Meed episode, and what yet lies ahead. A means of perfection, prayer is essentially the heart's uniting itself with God. Walter Hilton gives the classical definition:

For prayer is nothing but the rising of the heart to God leaving all earthly thoughts behind. And so it is compared to fire which of its nature springs up into the air. In the same way prayer, when it is enkindled by God's spiritual fire, is always rising up to Him from whom it came.[11]

Hilton also discusses the classical three degrees of prayer by which the spiritual progress of the soul toward union with God is marked off into stages. The first degree is vocal prayer, which includes Will's *pater-noster* and thus indicates that he is still in the early stages of conversion:

You must know that there are three degrees of prayer. There is first vocal prayer, either given us directly by God Himself, as the *Pater-noster,* or by the Church, as matins, vespers, and the other canonical hours, or else composed by holy men and addressed to our Lord, our Lady, or the saints ... Generally speaking this kind of prayer is most suitable in the early stages of conversion.[12]

What yet lies ahead for Will is indicated by the remaining two degrees of prayer, commonly called affective or meditative prayer and prayer of contemplation.[13]

[11]   *Scale,* I, 25, p. 37.
[12]   *Ibid.,* I, 27, pp. 38-39.
[13]   For a full discussion of prayer in itself and as a means of perfection according to medieval spiritual writers generally, see Garrigou-Lagrange, *op. cit.,* pp. 199-221.

The second degree of prayer is vocal, but without any set formula. This is when a man by the grace of God feels devotion, and out of his devotion speaks to Him as though he were bodily in His presence, using such words as come to mind and seem to be in accord with his feelings . . . This kind of prayer is very pleasing to God for it comes straight from the heart, and for that reason it is never made in vain. It belongs to what I have called the second degree of contemplation.[14]

The third degree of prayer is in the heart and without words. It is characterized by great peace and rest in soul and body. The man who would pray in this manner must have great purity of heart, for it is only possible to those who, either by long spiritual and bodily excercise, or else by sudden movements of love . . ., have come to great inward peace . . . This peace our Lord gives to some of His servants as a reward for their labour and a foreshadowing of the love which they shall have in the happiness of heaven.[15]

In order to offer Christ the prayers of a perfect man, to bring his will into conformity with God's will, and to begin a time when all shall turn to profit, Will must achieve contemplation and the unitive life.

Such is he who asks Lady Church how he may save his soul. His question itself is charged with his characteristic fervor and singleminded concern for his soul's welfare:

> Thanne knelede ich on my knees . and criede hure of
>   grace,
> And preiede hure pytously . to preie for me to amende,
> Al-so to kenne me kyndelich . on crist to by-leue,
> 'And teche me to no tresour . bote telle me thys ilke,
> How ich may sauy my saule . that seynt art yholde.'

                                                     (II:76-80)

There are actually three requests here, the first two providing a context for the third, and all three consistent with a desire for salvation through perfection rather than an ordinary state of grace. That Will desires to amend does not exclude him from the school of the perfect, for the need to amend is as real for the saintly as for the ordinary Christian, and a great deal more of

---

[14]   *Scale,* I, 29-30, pp. 41-42. Hilton's second degree of contemplation is equivalent to meditation.
[15]   *Ibid.,* I, 32, pp. 44-45.

a problem because of the degree of purity sought. Nor is it inconsistent with the degree of Will's preexisting goodness or his need to be converted – any more than it is inconsistent that St. Bernard's treatise on conversion was addressed to persons already in the religious state, or that much of Richard Rolle's or Walter Hilton's teaching on these matters was addressed to anchoresses. The way of perfection is a way unto itself, and it begins at the beginning. It does not require that at the outset one be either in danger of damnation or already in a state of grace.[16] It is for those who are imperfect, but have the capacity for perfection. As Dom Gerard Sitwell has pointed out, conversion is basically "the complete orientation of life to God ... It could imply merely the change from a good to a better form of life." [17] And as St. Bernard describes the first step of conversion, discussed in the previous chapter, it is a matter of understanding one's own sinful nature and of scrutinizing the memory to bring to light all the accumulated stains left by sins committed over one's whole life, even though the sins themselves may have been abandoned:

For, however quickly passed all the prurience of sinful flesh, however soon ended all voluptuous charm, it impressed the thoughts of its bitterness upon the memory; it left its foul traces.[18]

Will is a good man by ordinary standards, but he still finds Lady Meed seductive, and he will not be relatively invulnerable to temptation until he achieves perfection.[19]

That this desire to amend is expressed by one who seeks perfection is indicated by the request that immediately follows: to understand (and "kyndelich") how to live in Christ. The phrase "on crist to byleue" does not mean to learn the articles of faith about Christ, but to follow Christ, to be spiritually one with him.

---

[16] St. Thomas discusses problems relevant to this point in his *Apology for the Religious Orders,* trans. by The Very Rev. Father John Proctor, S.T.M. (London, 1902), chap. 6.
[17] *Scale,* p. 39, n. 2.
[18] *Of Conversion,* p. 6.
[19] Thus in *Dobest* Will is not seduced by anything he sees. Nor is Conscience, despite the severity and subtlety of the attacks against him.

The A- and B-texts make this clear by including one line not included in C:

> And ek kenne me kyndely . on crist to beleue,
> þat I miȝte werchen his wil . þat wrouȝte me to man:
>
> (A, I:79-80)

> And also kenne me kyndeli . on criste to bileue,
> That I miȝte worchen his wille . that wrouȝte me
> to man;
>
> (B, I:81-82)

The omission of the line in C does not alter the sense, for it is clear from passus 1, as well as the rest of the poem, that Will is not an unbeliever.[20] The significance of Will's desire to follow Christ is that following Christ constitutes perfection. The distinction between the means to ordinary goodness and the means to perfection is based on Matthew 19:16-21:

And behold, a certain man came to him and said, "Good Master, what good work shall I do to have eternal life?" He said to him, "Why dost thou ask me about what is good? One there is who is good, and he is God. But if thou wilt enter into life, keep the commandments." He said to him, "Which?" And Jesus said, "Thou shalt not kill, thou shalt not commit adultery, thou shalt not steal, thou shalt not bear false witness, honor thy father and mother, and, thou shalt love thy neighbor as thy self." The young man said to him, "All these I have kept: what is yet wanting to me?' Jesus said to him, "If thou wilt be perfect, go, sell what thou hast, and give to the poor, and thou shalt have treasure in heaven; and come, follow me."[21]

---

[20] Conrad Pepler, *op. cit.*, pp. 45-47, has characterized Will, before conversion, as being within the faith but spiritually dead, in that his faith is not at the very center of his life, or is only fitfully at the center. His conversion consists in his faith becoming a vital force to which all his other interests are subordinated. This psychological re-orientation, Pepler says, takes place in the Cornhill conversation. For my part, I find Pepler's description of Will's spiritual condition illuminating, but I cannot agree that Will's conversion begins on Cornhill. Pepler omits to consider the change Will undergoes as the result of Lady Church's teaching and the Meed episode.

[21] Donaldson, *op. cit.*, pp. 160-61, quotes this passage in order to suggest: "The *Visio*, with its picture of contemporary society, deals, much of the time by contrast, with the practical and social aspects of the first response:

Will does not ask about the commandments. His background of education and faith is tantamount to his saying, "All these I have kept: what is yet wanting to me?" His request corresponds to Christ's call to perfection achieved by means of the counsels. St. Thomas explains Christ's second statement: "In this saying of our Lord something is indicated as being the way to perfection by the words, *Go, sell all thou hast, and give to the poor:* and something else is added wherein perfection consists, when he said, *And follow Me.*"[22] The same scriptural passage is behind Richard Rolle's exhortation to a nun of Yeddingham, an exhortation that, according to one manuscript, is Rolle's whole message:

Crist couaytes þi fairehede in saule, þat þou gyf hym halely þi hert: and I preche noght ellys bot þat þou do his will, and afforce þe day & nyght to lefe alle fleschely luf and al likyng þat lettus þe to luf Ihesu Crist verrayly; for I-whils þi hert is heldande to luf of any bodyly thyng, þou may not parfitly by cupilde with god.[23]

The desire to do Christ's will is also central to Walter Hilton's

---

Keep the commandments. The *Vita,* a consideration of the degrees of perfection attainable by the individual, is a dramatization of the second response, which begins, *If thou wilt be perfect.*" In the previous chapter I have argued against the view that the *Visio* concerns society, the *Vita,* the individual. Social criticism is not confined to the *Visio,* and the question of salvation, which is the issue throughout the poem, is the concern of the individual. The present chapter, and all chapters hereafter, argue against the view that the *Visio* concerns salvation, the *Vita,* perfection. The call to obligatory goodness is applicable to those working in the world and thus may operate in the poem simultaneously with the call to perfection, but not separately. Nor does it govern the first part of the poem while perfection governs the second part. The way to goodness and the way to perfection are two different ways. Although the latter subsumes the former, it does not begin where the former ends, and for one who has the capacity and the vocation to achieve perfection, and commits himself thereto, there is no point at which he may cease to strive on the grounds that he has done enough to achieve salvation. From its very beginning *Piers Plowman* is governed by the call to perfection and divided according to stages in the single way of perfection, not according to the two different ways preached by Christ. If the latter were the case, then *Piers* would indeed, in all three texts, comprise a pair of companion but separate pieces.

[22] *Sum. Theo.,* II-II, q. 184, a. 3, rep. obj. 1.
[23] *Ego dormio et cor meum vigilat,* in C. Horstman, *Yorkshire Writers* (London, 1895), vol. I, p. 50, col. 2.

doctrine.[24] Hilton devotes six chapters to the necessity of seeking
Christ if one wishes to be perfect,[25] and his opening statement
corresponds in spirit to that just quoted from Rolle. It also reminds
us of Will's awareness that the soul is a saintly thing, of his
desire for nothing but the thing itself ("thys ilke"), and of his
life's being a life of prayer.

I am sure that anyone who had once a little insight into the dignity
and beauty which belong to the soul by nature and which it may
have again by grace, would hate and despise all that happiness and
love and beauty of this world as he would a piece of carrion. And his
only desire night and day – but for the frailty and the bare necessities of his bodily nature – would be to lament and seek by prayer
how he might come to it again. But inasmuch as you have not yet
seen fully what it is, because your spiritual eyes are not yet opened,
I will give you one word which shall comprise all the object of your
endeavours, for it contains all that you have lost. This word is
Jesus.[26]

Thus Will's desire to be directed to no treasure (the term Christ
used above, and specifically in connection with perfection), but
be told how he may save his soul is only one part of his question.
It must therefore be understood in light of the whole statement
rather than as if it were the only request made. In wishing to
amend and to know how to follow Christ, he indicates that he
is disposed to perfection in both desire and knowledge: in seeking to know the means, he indicates his intention actually to
achieve it.

His question, furthermore, must be understood in light of Lady
Church's reply. Together with Will's background, her reply is
also part of the context in which the central issue of *Piers Plowman* is raised. And since she personifies the Church itself, and
thus is meant to speak with ultimate and infallible authority in
matters of the spirit, her answer not only helps define Langland's

[24] At one point Hilton says: "Indeed I would rather have a true and pure
desire of Jesus in my heart, though with very little spiritual enlightment,
than practise all the bodily mortification of all men living, enjoy visions
and revelations of angels, or experience the most pleasing effects in my
bodily senses, if they were without this desire" (*Scale*, I, 47, p. 75).
[25] Chapters 46-51 in Book I of the *Scale*.
[26] *Ibid.*, I, 46, pp. 72-73.

conception of salvation, but also lays down the fundamental theological principles on which the development of *Piers Plowman* rests. The twofold importance of her statement warrants that it be given separate treatment.

IV. LADY CHURCH AND HER COUNSEL OF PERFECTION

Our examination of Lady Church's answer to Will must take two facts into account. The first is that since *Piers Plowman* is governed by the interior progress of the soul with Will as the focusing and dramatic personality, and since at the time of Lady Church's conversation Will is but embarking on the way, her reply comprises only what is profitable for him to know at this point. Lady Church gives him guiding ideas, discussing only the essentials of the goal – the ultimate treasure and the principal means. The second fact is that Langland continually assumes knowledge on the part of his audience. The truth of this is most obviously indicated by his use of Latin quotations. Usually he leaves them untranslated, at times he incorporates into his own English only the key Latin words, at other times he starts a Latin quotation and leaves an *& cetera* and the reader's own knowledge to finish it.[1] Lady Church's answer itself assumes one

[1] Sister Carmeline Sullivan has analyzed these and other techniques in *The Latin Insertions and the Macaronic Verse in Piers Plowman* (Washington, D. C., 1932). – Langland's homely vernacular, Will's struggle for the kind of knowledge he seeks, and, let us confess, our inability to understand this poem have contributed to the view that Langland was a moderately learned man with an unsystematic mind, and that he wrote for a popular audience. But we cannot judge his mind until we achieve a settled understanding of his poem. Langland's learning is being quietly vindicated, in fact, by our having to resort to works of master theologians in order to throw light on his poem. David Fowler has recently argued that *Piers Plowman* was written by John Trevisa, a learned man indeed (*op. cit.*, chap. 7). Langland's audience is simultaneously being vindicated. J. A. Burrow has already rejected the view that Langland was a popular poet, claiming instead that his audience comprised both clerics and learned laymen ("The Audience of *Piers Plowman*", *Anglia*, LXXV:4, 1957, pp.

sees how her teaching is based on the *Deus caritas* text, knows
in what sense a man becomes like God (and has in mind the
gospel passage and the words of St. Luke to this effect), and
understands how it is that man naturally loves God. These are
complex theological ideas; yet they are presented casually and,
except for the last idea, without elaboration.

In view of these two facts, we must expect Lady Church's
answer to be only a compendium of fundamental ideas. Rather
than dismiss these ideas as simple and popularly known, we must
take them seriously and fill them out. And in view of existing
scholarship on this passage,[2] the difficulty of the statement itself,
and the fact that Will is no dullard, the danger to avoid is that
of under-interpretation. Wells maintains, for example, that Lady
Church

never tells the dreamer more than any child might be expected to
know. She reads him, as it were, his catechism, stating simply those
ideas upon which the whole of the Christian System rests: the doctrine of free will, of the depravity of the body, of obedience to God,
of charity and grace.[3]

This assumption, however, not only fails to elucidate her statement,
but so underestimates her teaching as to hinder understanding.
Or again, the doctrine that man naturally comes to love God
more than himself and that he wishes to die rather than commit
any deadly sin is not explained by Coghill's bare and easy statement:

373-84). I think it possible that Langland had a two-fold audience in mind,
corresponding to his two-fold intention. He may have aimed his random
social criticism at anyone who could listen, if not read, but his systematic
allegorical dramatization of the spiritual ascesis at individuals, such as
clerics, who had both a specialized knowledge of, and a specialized interest
in, such matters.

[2]   Father Dunning, *Interpretation of the A-Text,* pp. 42-67, gives careful
attention to Lady Church's answer, Robertson and Huppé, *op. cit.,* pp. 42-
48, only brief attention. For the rest, partly because scholars have been
more interested in the *Vita* than the *Visio,* Lady Church's answer has been
ignored or merely scanned. Father Pepler, for example, who places this
poem in the context of spirituality, as I do, does not discuss the Lady
Church passus at all.

[3]   "The Construction of *Piers Plowman*", pp. 129-30.

truth and love are known by simple intuition, by a natural recognition in the human heart.[4]

Besides being contradicted by the very context here,[5] Coghill's gloss would have raised more than a few medieval eyebrows.

Lady Church's explanation of how Will may save his soul covers well over half of passus 2 and is divided into two parts at the point where Will asks to know how truth grows (II:137-38). These two parts constitute parallel answers to the question of salvation, rather than a single answer divided in half, for each develops the principal goal to be achieved and the principal means of achieving it. Together they discuss salvation in its two-fold aspect. The first part discusses salvation in terms of truth, and thus deals with the psychological change which must take place in the individual's interior makeup; the second discusses salvation in terms of love, and thus deals with the virtues by which a soul is saved. But the re-ordering and reformation of the soul's faculties, which constitute the psychological change, and growth in virtue, the principle of which is love, occur simultaneously. Lady Church answers the question of salvation twice, but each time in respect to a different principle.

She begins the first part of her sermon by giving man's earthly goal the name of truth:

> 'Whanne alle tresours ben tried,' quath hue . 'treuthe
>   is the beste;
> Ich do hit on *Deus caritas* . to deme the sothe.
> Hit is as derworthe a druwery . as dere god him-selue.
> For he, is trewe of hus tonge . and of hus two handes,
> And doth the werkes therwith . and wilneth no man ille,
> He is a god by the gospel . and graunty may hele,
> And like oure Lord also . by seynt Lukys wordes.
>
>   (II:81-87)

It should be noted, first, that neither here nor elsewhere does Lady Church discuss the ordinary means of salvation: faith in the Creed, sorrow for sins, reception of the sacraments, and so on.

---

[4] *The Pardon of Piers Plowman,* p. 10.
[5] Lady Church's complaint that Will must have learned too little Latin in his youth (II:140) denies Coghill's "simple intuition" theory by asserting the necessity of instruction.

The liturgical and sacramental means of grace as the foundation of the spiritual life are presupposed, having just been taken care of, in effect, by the preceding statement that Will is already baptized and within the Church (II:72-75). The very absence of concern with these indicates that Langland is thinking about salvation on a level deeper than the ordinary and catechetical, and that there is considerable distance between the teaching of *Piers Plowman* and that of, say, *The Parson's Tale* or *Everyman*, where only the ordinary means of salvation are urged. In presupposing the liturgy and the sacraments, Langland joins Rolle, Hilton, the author of the *Cloud*, and mystics generally, who seldom mention them because they are understood to be necessary.[6]

Nor does Lady Church's discussion correspond to Christ's call to goodness: Will does not ask about how he may keep the commandments, and Lady Church does not discuss the commandments as a way to salvation. Like the liturgical and sacramental means to salvation, observance of the commandments is also assumed. The goal Will has set for himself is to do Christ's will, and the answer he receives explains how he may be "A god by the gospel ... / And like oure Lorde". And Will seeks to be taught "kyndelich" in order that he may become what he knows, for the treasure of truth is possessed by actually being a certain kind of person, one who is true in thought ("wilneth no man ille"), word ("trewe of hus tonge"), and deed ("and of hus two handes"). Truth is not what the intellect possessess, but what the whole man is. Lady Church's description of the true man is parallel to Rolle's description of one who truly loves God and goes in the way of perfection:

[6] Father Pepler notes that mystics, particularly the later ones, presuppose the necessity of the liturgical and sacramental side of the spiritual life, but he claims emphatically that Langland presupposes nothing. This is a curious observation in view of Lanland's discussing these matters only intermittently and briefly, and not at all in passus 2, where he is giving his basic answer to the question of how one may save his soul. That Pepler's evidence comes from scattered passages, and mostly from the *Vita,* already indicates that while these matters come in at times, they are not in the forefront as the means on which Langland concentrates. See Pepler's *English Religious Heritage,* pp. 52-60.

Wharfore, þat þou may luf hym treweli, vndirstonde þat his luf is proued in thre thynges: In thynkyng, in spekyng, in worchyng. / Change þi thoght fro þe world and cast hit holli on hym, and he schal norisshe þe. / Change þi mouth fro vnprofitable & worldli speche (& speke) of hym, and he schal comfort the. / Change þine honden fro werkis of vanites and lift þaim in his nome and worche only for his luf, and he schal resceyue þe. Do þus and þou lufes him trewly and þou ghost in þe wey of parfitnesse. [7]

Lady Church's answer takes accurate account of Will's question, and it explains what Will desires to know: the way to perfection.

The term *treuthe* is not explicitly defined in what Lady Church says. Her description of the true man, like Rolle's description, enumerates the proofs, or manifest operations, of truth in the individual, but it does not define the quality of truth itself. She assumes, correctly, that Will understands in what sense a man's tongue and hands are true, and Langland assumes the same understanding in his audience. Our task, therefore, is to determine the meaning of this term from its context in order to elucidate this passage itself and Langland's view of salvation.

In passus 1 and 2 the term *treuthe* refers to both heaven and earth, designating in each case a goal of ultimate value for man. Truth in the tower is the heavenly destiny man should seek (II:130-34), and truth on earth is the dearest of all man's treasures (II:81). One relationship between these two goals is that the earthly truth "is as derworthe a druwery" as Truth itself. Thus the two truths are not identical in essence, but from the point of view of man's salvation they are equal in value. The other relation is that earthly truth makes man like heavenly Truth.[8] The earthly goal, therefore, derives its meaning and value from the heavenly goal, God himself. As applied to God, *Truth* is fixed and absolute; as applied to man, *truth* names the quality

---

[7] *þe Commawndement,* in Horstman, *op. cit.,* I, p. 67, col. 2. Rolle is here addressing a nun of Hampole.

[8] Father Dunning, *op. cit.,* p. 44, takes the statement "He is a god by the gospel" to mean a son of God, claiming that 'a' in this line means 'of' and that this is frequently the case in *Piers.* But he gives no evidence to this effect, except to refer the reader to Skeat, II, p. 3, where I find no mention of this at all. Skeat, in fact, nowhere comments on this line as far as I can tell. But there is no need to substitute words here. As we shall see, the idea of man becoming like God is central to medieval spirituality.

in virtue of which man is raised, not to an identity with God, but to a conformity with him.[9] In Lady Church's answer, therefore, having *treuthe* means being "like God", and the work of salvation is that of man's bringing himself, through the use of his bodily and spiritual faculties, into conformity with God. A man must be true in order to be united with Truth.

A more specific idea of how truth brings man into conformity with Truth can be determined from the next passage, in which Lady Church explains the principal means by which this goal is achieved (II:88-136). She discusses the means in terms of scriptural events and contemporary social problems, but the single point she makes is that man's will must desire what God's will desires. Kings and knights, she says, must execute laws out of a desire to fulfill God's will, and must be confined in the use of their power by the limits of God's will (II:90-101). They should hold with those who have true action and not leave the true party in deference to "lordene love", that is, to the will of a human being, even that of their earthly lord. Nor should they cease to defend and fight faithfully for truth "in hope to lacche selver", which again is to direct their will toward an object inferior to God. Finally, they should hold trespassers until truth has judged them, rather than usurp the prerogative of divine judgment by substituting their own will for God's. God's will is the absolute rule of action, and to make one's own will one's law, which is what all the above cases boil down to, is to contradict, rather than conform to, God's will. This is precisely what happened at the fall of the angels, the first knights (II:102-29). The whole point of bringing in this celestial event is to remind the Dreamer that to turn one's will from God to self is pride, the sin of Lucifer which every man re-enacts who does not seek to do God's will. Lady Church concludes this passage, and the first half of her sermon, by summing up the role of the will in man's salvation. All who "worchen that wikked ys" shall dwell with wrong, and all who "han wel ywrought" shall go East-

[9]   That Langland has in mind a conformity between God and man rather than an identity is indicated by what he says. The phrase is not "he is God", but "he is *a* god", and Langland adds, "*like* oure Lorde also".

ward to dwell with Truth (II:130-31). Here, as throughout the
poem, the emphasis is on work, action, mental and physical
activity. Action springs from the will; the emphasis on work of
all kinds in *Piers Plowman* arises from Langland's centering his
whole spirituality on the dynamism of the will.

The central importance of the will is also suggested by the
name Langland gives to his narrator and unifying consciousness,
and by Langland's presenting the confrontation of God and man
in the first two passus as essentially a confrontation of wills.
Langland does not discuss God in himself, but only as he is
related to man as man's final end; and God is related to man
in what he wills for man's sake. When Conscience speaks to the
king in passus 1 (the Angel speaks in the B-text), it is to make
known God's will. The first statement Lady Church makes about
Truth concerns God's will:

> 'The tour up-on toft,' quath hue . 'Treuthe ys ther-ynne,
> An wolde that ȝe wrouthe . as hus word techeth.
>
> (II:12-13)

God desires man to worship him with his five wits; he commands
the elements to provide for man; he has commanded in common
food, drink, and clothing (II:12-20). The Incarnation was an
act of divine love, whose seat is the will, and it is love that
"the lawe shapeth" (II:158). In short, the God whom man
confronts is a God who creates, teaches, commands, judges,
punishes, loves: a God who wills and whose will is man's true
rule of action.[10]

On the side of man, it is also the will with which Langland is
principally concerned, and his other faculties secondarily insofar
as they are involved in making a choice. As man's promised
reward, God is the object of man's will rather than his intellect.
Lady Church sums up the whole vision of the Field of Folk
in two lines that characterize the problem as of the will:

> The most partie of the puple . that passeth on this erthe,
> Have thei worship in this worlde . thei willen no betere.
>
> (II:7-8)

---

[10]   *See Sum. Theo.,* I-II, q. 71, a. 6; and q. 74, a. 1, 2.

Asking how he may save his soul, Will seeks to know the direction his will should take, wishing to be directed to no treasure but the very thing itself (II:79).

The soul's movement toward Truth also depends on man's freedom. Man must choose between the Tower and the Dungeon, and it is in the hope of influencing man's free choice that God, the Angel, Conscience, and Reason instruct and admonish on one side, and the Devil and his crew urge and flatter on the other. Man stands between the Tower and the Dale in virtue of being free to will either alternative, to choose freely either good or evil. The human condition as Langland dramatizes it is similar to that described by St. Bernard:

Accordingly free will maketh us our own; evil will maketh us the devil's; good will maketh us God's . . . When, therefore, by reason of evil will we belong to the devil, in a certain sense we do not meanwhile belong to God; even as when by reason of good will we become God's possession, we then cease to be the devil's; seeing that "No man can serve two masters". For the rest, whether we belong to God or to the devil, we do not cease to belong to ourselves also. Indeed free will remaineth to us in either case, whereby there remaineth also the ground of merit; so that deservedly we are either punished as evil persons, who have of their own will freely become such, or glorified as good, which equally we cannot be save only as free agents. In truth it is our own will, and not the power of God, which delivereth us over to the devil: it is God's grace, and not our own will, which maketh us subject to God. Our will, of course, was (as must be confessed) created good by the good God; it will not, however, be perfect until it hath been perfectly subjected to its Creator . . . For if to will what is evil is, as it were, a failure of the will, then to will what is good must be a success of the will; for the will, however, to be able to will everything that is good is its perfection.[11]

The man who is true of tongue and hands and wills no man ill has submitted all of his bodily members and mental faculties to the regulation of his will, and his will, in turn, is "perfectly subjected to its Creator". Such a man, able to will everything that is good as far as possible on earth, has achieved perfection. St. Edmund Rich provides a bridge between St. Bernard's statement and Lady Church's:

[11] *Concerning Grace and Free Will*, trans. by W. W. Williams (London, 1920), pp. 31-32. Williams' translation is used throughout.

To live perfectly, as St. Bernard teaches us, is to live humbly, loving-
ly and honorably. To live honorably towards God is to intend
nothing except to do His will; and that means to do His will in everything, in the thoughts of your heart and the words of your mouth and
the deeds of your hands, in each of your five senses. Seeing, hearing,
tasting, smelling, touching, when you walk or stand, lie down or sit,
always begin by asking yourself, is this His will or not? [12]

Taken in the context of Langland's discussion, truth means to be
like God through a conformity of wills. Truth is not in respect
of the intellect, naming a conformity between the intellect and
God. Langland does not view salvation as achieved through knowledge, but through love. [13] Indeed, in the *Vita* he discusses at
length the issue of knowledge versus love as the means of salvation, and Piers himself, who Clergy says impugnes all forms
of knowledge except love, loyalty, and humility, adds his authority
to the argument (XVI:128-50). [14] Besides, man is not raised to
God by his intellect; rather God is drawn down to man and
limited by the bounds of man's ideas. [15] Truth is in respect of

---

[12] *The Mirror of Holy Church*, trans. by Eric Colledge, *The Mediaeval
Mystics of England* (New York, 1961), p. 125.
[13] The question of the superiority of love over knowledge where man's
salvation is concerned is of long-standing and major importance to mystics
because it involves the nature of perfection and of union with God. St.
Bernard's arguments earned him the reputation of being anti-intellectual,
just as Langland sometimes gives that impression. (See, for example,
Bernard's Sermon XXXVI on the *Canticle of Canticles*.) St. Thomas held
that while the intellect in itself is superior to the will, where man's relation
to God is concerned the will is superior to the intellect, for love of God is
superior to knowledge of God (*Sum. Theo.*, I, q. 82, a. 3). The German
mystics of the 13th and 14th centuries tended to emphasize the importance
of the intellect and developed a characteristically intellectual school of
mysticism. (See Gerard Sitwell, *Spiritual Writers of the Middle Ages*, New
York, 1961, pp. 75-88.) Modern theologians continue to argue this issue.
(See Garrigou-Lagrange, *op. cit.*, pp. 129-44.)
[14] Father Dunning has argued that the value of learning is *the* subject of
the A-*Vita* (*Interpretation of the A-Text*, pp. 167-86), and David Fowler
has extended this view to the B-*Vita* (*op. cit., passim*). This issue is but a
theme, however, which inevitably arises from the larger subject of the
mystical way to salvation. A full study of the *Vita* as a continuation of the
way begun in the *Visio* of all three texts should collapse their arguments.
It should also thereby collapse their view that the *Visio* and *Vita* in the
A-text are separate poems.
[15] *Sum. Theo.*, I, q. 82, a. 3.

the will, the outgoing faculty which is "inclined to the thing itself as existing in itself".[16] The term has an ethical sense in Langland rather than an ontological sense. Man is true when he is what he ought to be, and he is what he ought to be when his will conforms to God's will. *Truth* is synomous with *rectitude, righteousness, justice,* all of which express the fact that man's will desires what God's will desires.

> For He is the living and intelligent Rule of equity, inflexible and inevitable, because reaching everywhere, to Which no wickedness can oppose itself without being confounded. And how can it be but that everything inflated and everything distorted shall impinge upon It and be broken? But woe to whatever stands in the way of this Rectitude.[17]

> When, therefore, it is asked how that is just which is just, the most fitting answer will be: because it is according to the will of God, which is just.[18]

Using *truth* in this way, Langland is in the tradition of both St. Anselm and Bishop Grossteste, who define *truth* as *rectitudo,* the conformity between man's will and God's.[19] And Father Dunning's statement that " 'Truth' presupposes the uprightness of life described in [the "trewe of hus tonge" passage]" [20] is not accurate. *Truth* does not presuppose uprightness; it names the fact of uprightness.

This sense of truth is also evinced by the interchangeability of the terms *truth* and *love* in Lady Church's sermon. Although she begins the first part of her answer with the statement that truth is the best treasure, she speaks of both truth and love in her elaboration, and ends this part by saying, "Than treuthe and trewe loue . ys no tresour bettere" (II:136), thus making love as much a treasure as truth. Whereupon Will asks how *it* grows, rather than how *they* grow (II:137-58), again indicating the practical identity between the two. The second part of Lady

[16]   *Ibid.*
[17]   St. Bernard, *On Consideration,* trans. by a Priest of Mount Melleray (Dublin, 1921), V, xii, p. 185.
[18]   Hugh of St. Victor, *De Sacramentis,* trans. by R. J. Deferrari (Cambridge, Mass., 1951), I, iv, 1, p. 61.
[19]   See Fred. Copleston, *History of Philosophy* (London, 1950), vol. II, p. 61.
[20]   *Interpretation of the A-text,* p. 64.

Church's answer, initiated by Will's request, does not introduce
the idea of love as if for the first time, or as if it were distinct
from truth; rather it explains the same goal and the same
means of salvation according to another principle. Lady Church
concludes her answer, and this passus, finally, by again interchanging *truth* and *love*:

> Whenne all tresours ben tryed . treuth ys the best;
> Loue it,' quath that lady . 'lette may ich no lengere
> To lere the what loue ys' . and leue at me hue lauhte.
>
> (II:203-205)

The true man is the man who loves God, and as love is of the
will, so truth is of the will. *Truth* names the fact of the will's
conformity with God's, *love*, the act of the will's conforming
itself with God's. Love of God is charity, and charity, as Gilson
explains in his analysis of Bernard's mystical theology, "is the will
common to man and God. It reigns therefore in the heart when
our will desires what God's will desires." [21] The author of *The
Cloud of Unknowing* similarly defines "þis meek steryng of loue":

> It is not ell*es* bot a good & an acordyng wil vnto God,
> & a man*er* of weelpayednes & a gladnes þat þou felest
> in þi / wille of alle þat he doþ.
>   Soche a good wille is þe substau*n*ce of alle *p*erfec-
> cion.[22]

Thus according to both the principle of truth and the principle of
love, the work of salvation consists in bringing man's will into
conformity with God's.

The importance of understanding that *truth* refers to the will
is that it explains the sense in which the true man is like God
and Christ. The remote principle of likeness between God and
man, of course, is grace, since grace is participation in the very
deity of God. St. Thomas defines grace as "nothing short of a
partaking of the Divine Nature, which exceeds every other nature.
And thus it is impossible that any creature should cause grace.
For it is as necessary that God alone should deify, bestowing a

[21] *The Mystical Theology of St. Bernard,* trans. by A. H. C. Downes
(London and New York, 1940), p. 72.
[22] *The Cloud of Unknowing,* ed. by Phyllis Hodgson (London, 1944),
chap. 49, p. 92.

partaking of the Divine Nature by a participated likeness, as it
is impossible that anything save fire should enkindle." [23] Lady
Church names this remote principle by which man is deified:

> So loue ys lech of lyue . and lysse of alle peyne,
> And the graffe of grace . and graythest wey to heuene.
> For-thy ich may say, as ich seide . by syght of the tixt,
> Whenne alle tresours ben tryed . treuth ys the best;

(II:200-203)

but since her interest is in being as practical as she can, while
still keeping her discussion on the level of principle, she emphasizes the proximate principle: the union of man's will with God's.
There is no other sense in Christian doctrine in which the need
for man to achieve a likeness to God is a fundamental strategy
of salvation; and this view of man's approach to God was developed specifically by the mystics. The background of her answer
to Will is the doctrine of deification, which holds that through a
conformity of man's will with God's man becomes like God and
is thereby deified.[24] St. Bernard expresses this doctrine in an often
quoted passage from his *De Diligendo Deo:*

Since however, Scripture says God *hath made all things for Himself*
(Prov. xvi, 4), it will certainly come to pass that the creature will at
one time or another conform itself to its Author and be of one mind
with Him. We ought therefore be transformed into this same dis-
position of soul, so that as God has willed that everything should be
for Himself, so we too may deliberately desire neither ourselves nor
any other thing to have been in the past, or to be in the future, unless
it be equally for His sake, to wit, for His sole will, not for our own
pleasure. A need allayed, or good fortune received will not delight us
so much as that His will is seen perfectly fulfilled in us and by us;
which, too, is what we daily ask in prayer when we say: *Thy will be
done on earth as it is in heaven (Matt.* vi, 10). O love, holy and
chaste! O sweet and pleasing affection! O pure and undefiled intention of the will! the more surely undefiled and purer, as there is now
mixed with it nothing of its own; so much the sweeter and more
pleasing, as its every feeling is wholly divine. To be thus affected is

---

[23]   *Sum. Theo.,* I-II, q. 112, a. 1.
[24]   Discussions of this doctrine can be found in: W. R. Inge, *Christian
Mysticism,* Eighth edition (London, 1948), Appendix C, pp. 356-68; E. Under-
hill, *Mysticism,* Fourth edition (London, 1912), pp. 500-509; P. P. Parente,
The Mystical Life (St. Louis and London, 1946), pp. 163-69; and C. Butler,
Western Mysticism, Second edition (London, 1926), pp. 108-110.

to become deified. Just as a little drop of water mixed with a lot of wine seems entirely to lose its own identity, while it takes on the taste of wine and its color; just as iron, heated and glowing, looks very much like fire, having divested itself of its original and characteristic appearance; and just as air flooded with the light of the sun is transformed into the same splendor of light so that it appears not so much lighted up as to be light itself; – so it will inevitably happen that in the saints every human affection will then, in some ineffable manner, melt away from self and be entirely transfused into the will of God.[25]

The essential idea in Bernard's statement is the same as is found in Lady Church's. "Seek to conform your will to God's", both say in effect, "by extirpating all self-will in order to make God's will your sole rule of conduct. You may then become deified, that is, very like God, and you will thereby have the surest hope of salvation." Indeed, the Cistercian way of union with God, as Gilson characterizes it, is fundamentally identical with Langland's way of salvation:

The essential character of Cistercian mysticism is now plain: it rests wholly upon a conscious effort to perfect the natural likeness of the soul to God, by means of a conformity, ever more fully realized, between the human will and the divine will.[26]

---

[25] *On the Necessity of Loving God,* trans. by Terence Conolly, S. J., in Anton C. Pegis, *The Wisdom of Catholicism* (New York, 1949), pp. 255-56. All references to this work will be to Pegis's edition.

[26] *The Spirit of Mediaeval Philosophy,* trans. by A. H. C. Downes (New York, 1940), p. 300. – It would require a separate study to determine whether Langland belongs specifically to the Cistercian tradition, and such a determination may finally be impossible. The lines of transmission of medieval thought are confused and relatively little known. Then, too, Bernard's influence on the later Middle Ages was so pervasive as to be difficult to isolate. But several prominent facts about *Piers Plowman* suggest a strong Cistercian influence. Langland quotes not only Bernard, but also some of the major figures who influenced Bernard: Cicero, Augustine, Gregory, and especially St. Benedict and St. John. The *Deus caritas* text, in fact, provided a key 'bloc' of doctrine for Bernard as for Langland. (See Gilson, *Mystical Theology of St. Bernard,* pp. 1-32; and *Spirit of Mediaeval Philosophy,* pp. 289-303.) The practicality of Langland's teaching, his emphasis on work, suggests the fundamental Benedictinism of Cistercian spirituality. The absence of Dionysian terminology, such as is found in *The Cloud* and somewhat in Hilton, but not at all in Langland or in Bernard, also suggests a special affinity. And so on with other similarities that have already appeared or will appear later in this study.

V. THE DOCTRINE OF DEIFICATION

Both Greta Hort [1] and E. Talbot Donaldson [2] have observed the relevance of the doctrine of deification to *Piers Plowman*, but feeling that Langland merely tended toward this doctrine rather than built on it, each has observed its possible working only in certain parts of the poem. Their hesitance positively to affirm its presence arises from Langland's seemingly having omitted to formulate it. But Lady Church's definition of the way to salvation as becoming a god and like our Lord is as forthright a formulation as is required. Her statement is unelaborated, but again we must remind ourselves that Langland assumes knowledge in his audience, that Will is lacking in experience more than in learning, and that this statement is made at a time when Will's spiritual journey is being initiated. It remains for Will actually to undergo the changes that may be consummated in the soul's deification. And as Lady Church's statement expresses the basic ideas on which this poem rests, so the doctrine of deification is central to its entire development.

The idea of union with God through likeness is a key idea in Western mysticism, having its antecedents in the pagan mystery cults of both Greece and Rome. As reported by early Christian writers, the object of these cults "was to place the person, the *mystes*, in a special close, privileged relation with the divinity honored in that mystery. In time, this close relation with the divinity became a transformation into one or more of the divine attributes, a deification, and consequently the initiation came to

[1] *Op. cit.,* pp. 81, 115.
[2] *Op. cit.,* p. 186.

be regarded as a rebirth, a resurrection." [3] This may possibly be what Lady Church has in mind when, immediately after explaining that truth makes man a god, she adds:

Clerkus that knowen thys . shoulde kennen hit a-boute,
For cristene and vncristene . cleymen it echone.

(II:88-89)

For Christians, deification is justified by the Incarnation, for "He became man that we might be made God". [4] It is required by the beatific vision, for "We know that, when he shall appear, we shall be like to him: because we shall see him as he is" (I John 3, 2). The gospel passage to which Lady Church refers when she says, "He is a god by the gospel" (II:86), may be John 10:34-38, in which Jesus answers the charge of blasphemy for claiming that "I and the Father are one".

Jesus answered them, "Is it not written in your Law, 'I said you are gods'? If he called them gods to whom the word of God was addressed (and the Scripture cannot be broken), do you say of him whom the Father has made holy and sent into the world, 'Thou blasphemest,' because I said, 'I am the Son of God'? If I do not perform the works of my Father, do not believe me. But if I do perform them, and if you are not willing to believe me, believe the works, that you may know and believe that the Father is in me and I in the Father." [5]

Or it may be John 17:20-23, a passage from the Last Supper:

"Yet not for these only do I pray, but for those also who through their word are to believe in me, that all may be one, even as thou, Father, in me and I in thee; that they also may be one in us, that the world may believe that thou hast sent me. And the glory that thou hast given me, I have given to them, that they may be one, even as we are one: I in them and thou in me; that they may be perfected in unity, and that the world may know that thou hast sent me, and that thou has loved them even as thou hast loved me."

The passage in Luke to which Lady Church refers when she says, "And like oure Lorde also . by seynt Lukys wordes" (II:87),

---

[3] Pascal Parente, op. cit., pp. 4-5.
[4] St. Athanasius, De Incarn. Verbi, i, 108. Quoted by Underhill, loc. cit.
[5] The quotation "I said you are gods" comes from Ps. 82:6, and is a phrase often quoted to justify the concept of deification. See Inge, op. cit., p. 358.

may be Luke 6:40, a verse from the Sermon on the Mount: "No disciple is above his teacher, but when perfected, everyone will be like his teacher." [6]

Led by St. Bernard, the Cistercians gave this doctrine extensive development, and after them it was taken up frequently by spiritual writers.[7] Gilson sums up Bernard's position:

Faithful to the ancient Greek doctrine that only like knows like, St. Bernard affirms that the necessary condition of the soul's knowledge of God lies in the likeness it bears to God ... the immediate condition of the beatific vision will be a perfect likeness of man to God; ... this likeness is at present too imperfect to justify any pretension to the beatific vision ... the more our likeness to God increases, so much the more does our knowledge of God. The stages therefore on the road by which we opproach Him are those of the spiritual progress of the soul in the order of divine likeness. This progress is the work of the Holy Spirit, but takes place in our spirit, and thanks to it we draw nearer and nearer to this divine state in which the soul will see God as He is, because it will now be, not indeed what He is, but such as He is.[8]

Walter Hilton also developed this view of man's approach to God. The entire teaching of the *Scale*, in fact, rests on the doctrine of deification. In his opening statement Hilton defines the essence of perfection:

... turn both internally and externally to God, and conform yourself inwardly to His likeness by humility and charity and the other virtues, and so you will be truly converted to Him.[9]

The terminus of this conformation is "reform in faith and feeling", which means to be made over into the likeness of

---

[6] St. Paul's epistles offer many passages sanctioning the doctrine of deification. See, for example, Rom. 12:2; I Cor. 6:17; I Cor. 15:48-49; and 2 Cor. 3:18.

[7] See Butler, *loc. cit.,* See also Gerard Sitwell, *Spiritual Writers of the Middle Ages, passim,* in which are discussed the theological views of individual mystics from Cassian to the end of the 15th century. The importance of the idea of union with God through becoming like God is evident in almost all of these mystics, but it is particularly prominent after the Cistercians.

[8] *The Mystical Theology of St. Bernard,* pp. 92-93.

[9] *Scale,* I, 1, p. 3.

Christ so that, unlike the ordinary Christian, one achieves a conscious awareness of the presence of Christ in the soul.[10]

The possibility of man's becoming like God rests on the doctrines of Creation and Redemption. According to Genesis 1:26-27, man was created in the image and likeness of God. As the result of the Fall, man's divine similitude was obscured but not destroyed; hence, man can, and must, be restored to his original divine likeness. The work of the Redemption, however, was first necessary to make this restoration possible; indeed, Christ figures centrally in the creation of God's similitude in man, as well as in the restoration of that similitude. For man is not *the* image of God, but made *in* the image of God. Christ, the Word, the Father's generation of Himself, is the Image, and man is made in the image of the Word. Hence, man is an image of the Image of God:

But someone will say to me: 'Why do you join these two together? What relation is there between the Word and the soul?' Much in every way. In the first place, there is so close an affinity between the nature of the One and that of the other, that the One is the Image and Likeness of God, the other made after that image. In the second place, the resemblance that is between them is a witness of that affinity. For the soul has been created, not only after the image, but in the likeness of it.[11]

And since, strictly speaking, man is in the image and likeness of Christ, it is Christ alone who can restore the divine image in man: "for, in order that it might receive again its original form, it needed to be reformed from the same source from which it had been formed".[12] In his divine nature, the Word is the Person of the Trinity to whom the work of restoration properly belongs:

And, in truth, whom did such a work befit better than the Son of God? Who seeing that He is the effulgence of the Father's glory, and the essential form of His very being, upholding the universe by His word, manifested Himself, endowed with full power for the twofold work of restoring what was deformed and strengthening

[10]   The entire *Scale* develops this theme, but see II, 31-33, pp. 237-46.
[11]   St. Bernard, Sermon LXXXII, 2 on the *Canticle,* trans. by S. J. Eales London, 1869). This translation is used throughout.
[12]   St. Bernard, *Concerning Grace and Free Will,* X, p. 53.

what was weak; putting to flight the darkness of sin by the effulgence of His Godhead, and restoring wisdom; and by the virtue of
His word giving power against the tyranny of evil spirits.[13]

In his human nature, Christ is the model and source of aid for
the restoration of man's divine likeness on earth:

But in truth we need also the help of Him by whose example we are
incited to such conduct as this; in order, plainly, that by means of
Him we may be conformed unto Him, and be "transformed into
the same image from glory to glory, even as by the Spirit of the
lord".[14]

Medieval spiritual writers found various ways in which man
bears a similarity to God. Many, following St. Augustine, saw
in man's soul a trinity of powers – memory, reason, and will –
resembling the Trinity of Persons in God. According to Hilton,
for example, before the Fall man's memory or conscious mind
was wholly fixed on God, his reason or understanding was clear
and free from error in its judgments, and his will was pure in
loving God above all things. These three faculties resembled the
Father, Son, and Holy Spirit respectively. As the result of the
Fall, man became forgetful of God, ignorant about his true good,
and driven by love of self.[15] Hugh of St. Victor saw a trinity of
attributes in man – goodness, wisdom, and power – as the
counterparts of similar attributes in God.[16] St. Bernard asserted
the trinity of powers Hilton describes,[17] but like the Victorine,
also considered man's attributes. In his view, man's soul bore the
image of God in being great and righteous, the likeness of God
in being simple in essence, immortal, and free. Its greatness,
which is the soul's capacity for spiritual things, was not lost as
the result of the Fall; but its original righteousness, its desire for
spiritual things, was lost. The soul did not lose the simplicity of
essence by which it not only lived but could live happily and well,
but became subject to a life of duplicity, to fraud, pretence, and

13   *Ibid.*, pp. 52-53.
14   *Ibid.*, p. 56.
15   *Scale*, I, 43, pp. 63-65.
16   *De Sacramentis*, I, ii. 10-13.
17   See Sermon XL, 5, on the *Canticle*.

hypocrisy. Its immortality, never perfect because subject to change, became clouded by the onset of physical pain and death. Its freedom, persisting after the Fall, became confused by the soul's voluntary servitude to fleshly lusts.[18]

But according to all medieval spiritual writers who considered the way in which man is the image of God, and all Christian philosophers as well, it is not only the soul, but especially the summit, the fine point, the apex or ground of the soul that bears the divine image. St. Augustine and St. Thomas placed the image in the intellect at the point where human thought (*mens*) is open to the illumination of the divine Ideas; but St. Bernard placed it in Free Choice, which is indestructible, even by Original Sin, and thus reflects God's eternality.[19] Free Choice, *Liberum arbitrium*, is the faculty by which the soul has power to distinguish and choose between good and evil. Able both to discern and direct, it is both rational and voluntary. And since it is free to carry out its decisions into action, Free Choice makes man capable of merit or demerit according as his actions are good or evil.[20] In virtue of this power, man is distinguished from animals and is capable of salvation or damnation.[21]

Man has freedom of choice, or freedom from necessity, in that he is subject to no coercion, internal or external, which can make him consent to what he does not love. In this respect, man bears the image of God. But the scope of this freedom depends upon two other freedoms which constitute man's divine likeness. One is freedom of counsel, or freedom from sin, which rests on his ability to determine whether what he loves is morally profitable; the other is freedom of pleasure, or freedom from misery, for when he was able to choose freely what is morally profitable, he enjoyed virtual immunity from pain and punishment. Man has never lost his divine image, freedom of choice, but this image has been obscured and freedom of choice restricted by the loss of his divine likeness. As the result of the Fall, man's understand-

[18] Sermons LXXX and LXXXI on the *Canticle.*
[19] See Gilson, *Spirit of Medieval Philosophy,* pp. 210-12, 225.
[20] Sermon LXXXI, 6, on the *Canticle.*
[21] *Concerning Grace and Free Will,* chap. II.

ing became subject to error in determining what is morally expedient and allowable, thus he is no longer able to avoid sin.
Subject to sin, he is liable to pain and punishment, no longer
possessing freedom of pleasure.[22]

The total restoration of these freedoms is what man prays for
on earth and what he shall receive in heaven if, utilizing his
freedom of choice, he gradually regains part of his freedom of
counsel by liberating his judgment from the embroilments of the
flesh and extricating himself from servitude to sin. To restore the
original lustre of his image, in other words, thereby making it
acceptable to God, man must learn to love, for love is the principal act of the will. He must reestablish Free Choice as the ruler
of the body, since the body impairs judgment and lets in sin so
that bitterness rather than joy is the final reward. Free choice
must rule, furthermore, in a manner that imitates Christ's gover-
nance of the universe:

He came, therefore, the very essential form (of God), to Whom the
free choice (of man) has to be conformed: for, in order that it might
receive again its original form, it needed to be reformed from the
same source from which it had been formed. But the form is Wisdom; the conformation consisteth in the image doing that work in
the human body which the form doth in the whole world.[23]

Wisdom "reacheth from one end to another mightily, and sweetly
doth it order all things" (Wisd. 8:1): that is, the Word governs
omnipresently and omnipotently, with a tranquil will, ordaining
all things to their proper end.[24]

Therefore let free choice seek to rule its own body, even as Wisdom
ruleth the world; itself also reaching 'from one end to another
mightily" to wit, giving its commands to each sense and to each
member with such authority that it allow no sin to reign in its mortal
body, nor yield its members as weapons to iniquity, but rather present them for the service of righteousness. Thus no longer will the
man be the servant of sin, when he doeth not sin; from which indeed
set free, he will now begin to recover freedom of counsel and to
vindicate his dignity, while he clotheth himself with a likeness be-

[22] *Ibid.,* chap. VII.
[23] *Ibid.,* p. 53.
[24] *Ibid.,* pp. 53-54.

fitting the divine image in himself, yea, restoreth his ancient comely state. But let him take heed that he do this not less "sweetly" than "mightily"; that is to say, "not of sorrow or of necessity", which is but the beginning, and not the fulness of wisdom; nay, rather, with a ready and a cheerful will, which maketh a sacrifice accepted, seeing that "God loveth a cheerful giver'. And thus in all things he will follow the example of Wisdom, both withstanding vice "mightily", and being "sweetly" at rest in conscience.[25]

All of which is to say that in order to be saved, man's free will must conform to God's will and his body must be in proper relation to his soul. Then he will be true of tongue and hands and wish no man ill (II:84-85), and receive such a "gobet of hus grace" as to "bygynne a tyme, / That alle tymes of my tyme . to profit shal turne" (VI:100-101).

The psychology involved in the doctrine of deification, particularly as St. Bernard developed it, can be seen working in Langland. Bernard's concept of *Liberum arbitrium* immediately suggests, as it did to Donaldson,[26] Langland's introduction of a personification with the same name. But before we consider this personification let us observe briefly the light which Bernard's teaching throws on the Meed episode.

Literally, the Meed episode deals with establishing order in the commune; but allegorically it dramatizes the first step of conversion in which the soul examines its sinfulness and judges itself at its own bar. The connection between the literal and allegorical is that both public disorder on the one hand, and the soul's alienation from God on the other, are caused by self-will, *voluntas propria*, as opposed to common will, *voluntas communis*.[27] The former seeks only its own, and thus is essentially cupidity; the latter seeks what is common to good men and God, and thus is essentially charity.[28] "In an earthly kingdom", St. Thomas

---

[25] *Ibid.,* pp. 55-56.

[26] *Op. cit.,* pp. 187-96.

[27] See St. Bernard, Third Sermon for Easter, in *St. Bernard's Sermons for the Seasons & Principal Festivals of the Year,* trans. by a Priest of Mount Melleray (Westminster, Maryland, 1950), vol. II, pp. 201-203. Hereafter cited as *Sermons.* See also Gilson, *The Mystical Theology of St. Bernard,* pp. 55-58.

[28] St. Bernard, Third Sermon for Easter, in *Sermons,* II, pp. 201-202.

says, "peace ceases when the citizens seek each man his own".[29] The truth of this is dramatized in passus 4 in which the officials of the court readily prefer Lady Meed's gifts to the cause of just arbitration, but especially in passus 5 where Peace himself prefers private gain to justice. In the end all agree to expel Lady Meed (Worldly Promises), thereby resolving to subordinate self-will to the common will. At the same time, the Meed episode dramatizes what takes place at the beginning of conversion: the rejection of carnal desire or cupidity (Lady Meed's allegorical significance) which feeds self-will, and a resolution to close the mortal body to sin.[30]

From the point of view of the doctrine of deification, the Meed episode dramatizes the soul's resolving to re-establish the rule of Free Will over the mortal body in order to regain freedom from sin, also called freedom of counsel, and to restore its divine image. For "Propyr wille", as a Middle English treatise on this subject puts it, is thoroughly opposed to God's will, while "commen wille" is "acordant wyht goddis wylle, and alle gode mens wille".[31] Common will, this treatise goes on to say, is the temple of God, the chamber of Jesus, the house of the Holy Ghost. It bears a likeness to the Trinity: "Of þe faydyr in fayrenes, of þe sone in mekenes, of þe haligast in gudenes." [32] Proper will, on the other hand, is completely unlike God's will, "for fendys dwellys þerin".[33] Whoever loves only himself hates God, forsakes the help of Holy Church, and offers himself to the fiends in Hell. To live according to proper will, in other words, is to live in what medieval spiritual writers called the *Regio dissimilitudinis*, the Land of Unlikeness, a state in which the soul still bears the loss of its divine similitude and thus is remote from God.[34] Gilson sums up the meaning of this notion:

---

[29]   *Sum. Theo.*, II-II, q. 183, a. 2, rep. obj. 3.
[30]   See St. Bernard, *Of Conversion*, chaps. 1-6.
[31]   Anonymous, "Propyr Wille", in Horstman, *op. cit.*, I, pp. 173-75. Quotations from p. 173.
[32]   *Ibid.*
[33]   *Ibid.*, p. 174.
[34]   For discussions of the history of this concept, see Etienne Gilson, "Regio Dissimilitudinis" de Platon à St. Bernard de Clairvaux", *Mediaeval*

Disfigured by original sin, man has in fact exiled himself from the Land of Likeness to enter into the Land of Unlikeness: *Regio dissimilitudinis*. There we have the first inversion of order from which all the evil has arisen. Conversion reversed, conversion for ever "execrable", by which man exchanged the glory of the Divine image for the shame of the earthly image, peace with God and with himself for war against God and against himself, liberty under the law of charity for slavery under the law of his own self-will. We might go still further and say that man, by that conversion, has exchanged heaven for hell; a word in which all the foregoing is summed up, for hell is at once self-will, and its consequence, unlikeness to God, and war set up between creature and Creator. Now this evil that Adam brought into the world is hereditary, and the proper object of the Christian life is to wage war on its effects ... If cupidity draws us on endlessly and inevitably from finite goods to finite, this is because man's nature is no longer in the state in which it ought to be; each man born henceforth is born deformed.[35]

When Will asks "to knowe the false" (III:4), he desires to see the interior man in a state directly opposed to that which makes him true, a god on earth and like our Lord: the man in whom the divine likeness is completely obscured. The reason Will seeks to know the false is that the sight of the soul's indignity, in contrast to the dignity it has in virtue of being created like God, makes the individual resolve to restore his original likeness.[36] Lady Church directs Will's attention to his "lyft half" (III:5), to the side of the body,[37] where he may see the interior man, out of love of self, bringing himself to the brink of damnation:

> Know hym wel, yf thow kanst . and kep the fro hem alle
> That louyeth hure lordsheps . lasse other more.
>
> (III:47-48)

The spirits of Hell have already infiltrated the thoughts (False and his gang), bodily affections (the various folk) are eager for

Studies, IX (1947), 108-30; and Pierre Courcelle, "Tradition néo-platonicienne et traditions chrétiennes de la "région de dissemblance," *Archives d'histoire doctrinale et littéraire du Moyen Age*, XXIV (1957), 5-33.
[35] *Mystical Theology of St. Bernard*, pp. 45-46.
[36] See St. Bernard, Sermon LXXXII, 7, on the *Canticle*.
[37] The allusion here is to Psalm 90, verse 7: "Though a thousand fall at your side, ten thousand at your right side, near you it shall not come." Bernard assigns the goods of the body to the left side, the goods of the soul to the right (Seventh Sermon on Psalm XC in *Sermons*, I, pp. 186-87).

gratification, and both seek to secure their ends by establishing a permanent bond between carnal desire (Lady Meed) and the corrupted mind. By the union of these two, thought and desire, the two sources of all sin, the affections hope to have free reign and the fiends hope to confirm the soul's damnation (the charter of marriage).

The attempt to marry carnal desire to corrupted thoughts takes place outside Westminster and out of the view of the King (Free-Will) because the lower nature of the soul in this state seeks its ends outside the law, seeks to be, indeed, its own law.[38] But the marriage cannot be accomplished, on the other hand, without the consent of the lawmaker, Free-Will, by which alone an interior motion is transformed into act.[39] All interested parties must inevitably, therefore, agree to Theology's directive to repair to the King's court to win consent. The vices and Lady Meed ride to the court on the backs of the folk (III:175-99) because the man who is free but unlike God has conformed himself to beasts:

What shall I say of the fact that a creature who is free does not subdue appetite and rule it as a queen, but, on the contrary, follows and obeys it as a servant? Does not such a creature rank itself among animals without reason, and make itself like unto them whom their nature has not called to liberty, but has placed in a state of servitude, to follow and obey their lusts and appetites?[40]

And the vices flee under threat of the King (III:200-252), finally, because the sinful soul, desiring to be its own law, fears the law which would command it to give up its vices. The first passus of the Meed episode, in short, describes allegorically the condition of the soul living in the Land of Unlikeness, the point from which the soul moves in its quest for perfection through re-establishing its divine similitude. And since the depiction here is for Will's benefit, and is, in fact, of Will's own soul, or the soul of any individual embarking on the way of perfection, the first passus of this episode not only describes the soul's condition, but also

[38]   St. Bernard, *On the Necessity of Loving God*, XIII, pp. 263-64.
[39]   St. Bernard, *Concerning Grace and Free Will*, XII, p. 69. See also Richard of St. Victor, *De Statu Interioris Hominis, Tractatus Primus,* in Migne, *P.L.,* vol. 196, coll. 1117B-1146B.
[40]   St. Bernard, Sermon LXXXII, 6, on the *Canticle*.

dramatizes how it begins to move out of its corrupted state. The only way it can rise above its deformity is through the intervention of grace, and this intervention is depicted by the appearance of Theology (III:116-54). God's grace comes to men in many ways, St. Bernard says, one of which is to enlighten the soul by means of Sacred Scriptures.[41]

Moving to the court, we move to the higher realm of the soul. The King, as Father Dunning has noted, represents Free-Will,[42] uncorrupted by the Fall but not in control, and Conscience and Reason are the two powers involved in freedom of counsel. Reason determines what is morally expedient, and thus is characterized as the King's "chyf chaunceler . in chekyr and in parlement" (V:185); Conscience determines what is morally allowable, thus is characterized as the "kynges Iustice" (V:186). Together, Reason and Conscience counsel the Kyng concerning what is morally profitable. The central issue is still "Which a maister Mede was . a-mong poure and riche" (V:26), but now it is up to the King to choose between Meed on the one hand, and Conscience with Reason on the other. At one point he is willing to accept the service of both Meed and Conscience (V:1-3), but after Reason is summoned, and it is seen how willingly Meed goes to the aid of Wrong and to the corruption of Peace (V:90-93), the King, acting on the advice of Conscience, resolves to show no mercy toward Wrong unless Reason counsels otherwise:

> 'Nay, by Crist,' quath the kynge . 'for Consciences
>   sake,
> Wrong goth nat so away . ar ich wite more;
> Loupe he so lyghtlich . lauhen he wolde,
> And eft be the boldere . to bete myne hewes;
> Bote Reson haue reuthe of hym . he shal reste in
>   stockes
> As longe as ich lyue . for hus luther werkes.'

(V:99-104)

Reason agrees that no mercy should be shown until a list of wrongs he mentions no longer takes place (V:108-130), which

---

[41] Eleventh Sermon on Psalm XC, in *Sermons,* I, pp. 231-32.
[42] *Interpretation of the A-Text,* pp. 101-102.

means, from the point of view of the allegory, that no mercy
should be shown the affections until sin no longer reigns in the
body. Reason concludes by saying that if he were king . . .

> That ich were kyng with corone . kepe eny reame,
> Shold neuere wronge in this worlde . that ich wite
>   myghte,
> Be vnpunysshed in my power . for peril of my soule,
> Ne gete me grace thorw eny gift . ne glosyng speche,
> Ne thorw mede do mercy . by Marye of heuene!
> For man, *nullum malum* . mette with *impunitum*,
> And bad that *nullum bonum* . bee *irremuneratum*.

> (V:135-41)

Reason's speech says allegorically what St. Bernard says literally
in the first part of the passage already quoted:

Therefore let free choice seek to rule its own body, even as Wisdom
ruleth the world; itself also reaching "from one end to another
mightily" to wit, giving its commands to each sense and to each
member with such authority that it allow no sin to reign in its
mortal body, nor yield its members as weapons to iniquity, but
rather present them for the service of righteousness.

After considering Reason's statement, the whole commune is converted against Meed; she is expelled, and the King swears to take
Reason and Conscience as his counselors. Thus the first stage
of conversion, and the first step toward regaining man's natural
likeness to God, is accomplished; but only the first step, for the
body is far from perfectly subdued, and the King and the coun-
sellors have been stern and merciless. The soul has judged itself
mightily, but must learn to govern itself sweetly as well:

But let him take heed that he do this not less "sweetly", than
"mightily"; that is to say, "not of sorrow or of necessity", which is
but the beginning, and not the fulness of wisdom.

The outcome of the Meed episode is only a resolution to subdue
the body, not its actual subjugation. The remainder of the *Visio*
dramatizes the problems of bringing the body more permanently
to heel, enough at least to enable the soul to begin progress in the
spiritual life properly so-called. The *Dowel* section of the *Vita*
dramatizes the soul's eradicating the deepest propensities to sin,
both mortal and venial, or what Walter Hilton calls the "image

of sin" that has overlaid man's divine image with the likeness
of a beast.[43] This foul image is, again, essentially self-love and is
subdued when love of self is replaced by humility and charity:
deprecation of self and love of God.[44] By the end of *Dowel* the
last remnants of self-love are being overthrown so that charity
may then become the soul's concern. At this point, after a long
eulogy on poverty (XVII:117-57), the divine image in man
appears, and not under the allegorical guise of a king, but plainly
and under its own name of *Liberum Arbitrium* (XVII:158-XIX:
180). *Liberum* speaks two lines that sum up the whole case
against self-love:

> 'He that hath londe and lordshep,' quath he . at the laste
>   ende
> Shall be pourest of power . at hus partyng hennes.'
>
> (XVII:160-61)

Will immediately seeks to know "what he was" (XVII:162), and
the answer he receives characterizes *Liberum* in a way fundamentally identical with Bernard's conception, and in the context of
the doctrine of deification. *Liberum* begins by explaining that he
is Christ's creature, known in Christ's court and a member of
Christ's kin:

> Is nother Peter the porter . ne Paul with his fauchon,
> That wolde defende me heuene dore . dynge ich neuere
>   so late.
> At my-ny3t, at mydday . my uoise is so yknowe,
> That eche creature that loueth Christe . welcometh me
>   faire.'
>
> (XVII:169-72)

Liberum Arbitrium, in other words, is the point of contact
between the soul and God, and the faculty to which the salvation
of the soul is specifically ascribed. *Liberum's* explanation of himself is essentially the same as Bernard's:

What, therefore, thou askest, doth free will do? I answer in a word:
It is saved. Take away free will and there remaineth nothing to be
saved; take away grace and there is no means whereby it can be
saved. This work of salvation cannot be wrought without two fac-

[43] *Scale,* I, 50-92, pp. 80-138.
[44] *Ibid.,* 51, p. 81; 92, pp. 137-38.

tors: the one, that by which it is wrought, and the other, that for which or in which it is wrought ... Accordingly free will is said to co-operate with the grace which worketh salvation, when the free will consenteth, that is to say, is saved; for to consent is to be saved.[45]

Liberum Arbitrium then explains his function as the faculty which freely chooses between good and evil, and defines himself, as St. Bernard defines Free Choice, as a faculty that is both voluntary and rational:

> 'Wher-of serue ȝe?' ich seide . 'syre *Liberum-arbitrium?*'
> 'Of som tyme to fyghte,' quath he . 'falsnesse to destruye,
> And som tyme to suffre . bothe sorwe and teene,
> Layke other leue . my lykynge chese,
> To do wel other wikke . a wil with a reyson,
> And may not be with-oute a body . to bere me wher hym
>   lyketh.'
>
> (XVII:173-78)

The last line of this statement raises a point which Will is quick to grasp: if inseparable from a body which follows its own will, then Free Choice has a qualified freedom. This difficulty is easily resolved, but in the course of resolving it, *Liberum* reveals that he is apparent only in a perfect man, one whose free will agrees with God's will, and whose carnal will is subject to his free will. In such a man Free Choice governs "sweetly" as well as "mightily":

> 'Thenne is that body bettere than thow', quath ich .
>   'nay' quath he, 'no betere;
> Bote as a wode were a fure . thenne worchen thei bothe,
> And ayther is otheres heete . and also of a wil;
> And so is man that hath hus mynde . myd *Liberum-
>   arbitrium.*'
>
> (XVII:179-82)

Finally, that *Liberum Arbitrium* is the focal-point of the soul is clear when he goes on to explain all his other names, which are the names of all the operations of the soul, including that of the vegetative soul *(Anima)*, those of the animal soul *(Animus* and *Sensus)*, the rational soul *(Memoria, Racio, Conscientia,* and *Liberum-arbitrium* itself), and those of the soul in its entirety

[45]   *Concerning Grace and Free Will,* pp. 4-5.

(Amor and *Spiritus)* (XVII:183-201). These are all *Liberum's* names because as the ground of man's soul he is the ground of all operations. And there is no irony intended when Will, after hearing all of these names, says *Liberum* is like a bishop, for *Liberum* answers simply and soberly, "That is soth" (XVII: 206). Free Choice is indeed like a bishop because it stands at the head of the hierarchy of operations in the soul and has jurisdiction over all the powers beneath it.

Having explained himself, *Liberum Arbitrium* reprimands Will for intellectual pride, quoting St. Bernard along the way:

> Beatus, seith seynt Bernard . *qui scripturas legit,*
> *Et uerba uertit in opera* . emforth his power,
> (XVII:221-22)

thus ridding Will of the last obstacle in the way of true humility (XVII:212-85). This sermon brings up the subject of charity, and Will immediately asks "wher may hit be founde?" (XVII:285). *Liberum's* discourse on charity extends through the remainder of passus 17 and all of 18, forming the transition between *Dowel* and *Dobet.* At the beginning of passus 19, he leads Will to charity's dwelling, which is man's own heart, in the center of which grows *Ymago-dei* (XIX:1-7), and begins the series of visions that culminate in the visions of Christ and the Paraclete.

VI. LADY CHURCH AND HER SECOND ANSWER

In psychological terms, the doctrine of deification describes salvation as consisting in the restoration of the soul's powers or attributes in general, and its divine spark in particular, to their original integrity so that the soul once more bears a likeness to God. Progress toward likeness and union with God, however, also requires virtue, for the soul moves toward God through the progressive acquisition of virtue:

Thus the more pure and vigorous a spirit is, the nearer it is to God, and to have attained absolute purity and virtue is to have come into the very Presence of God. For to be in His Presence is to see Him as He is; and to do this is nothing else than to be as He is, and so not to be dazzled and confounded by being unlike Him.[1]

The virtue ultimately aimed for is charity, for love is the bond of union between the soul and God:

to be reformed by Him, and to be rendered conformable to Him. In what respect? In charity ... It is that conformity which makes, as it were, a marriage between the soul and the WORD, when, being already like unto Him by its nature, it endeavours to show itself like unto Him by its will, and loves Him as it is loved by Him.[2]

Charity is also the principle of all virtues; to achieve perfect charity is to possess all virtues perfectly, thus to be conformed to God in virtue. The soul united to God in the Unitive Life possesses virtues without being concerned about them, for in this state "Love is filled with itself; and in the soul to which it has once come, it overcomes and transforms all other feelings. There-

---

[1] St. Bernard, Sermon XXXI, 3, on the *Canticle*.
[2] *Idem,* Sermon LXXXIII, 2-3, on the *Canticle*.

fore the soul which loves, in loving, is regardless of all else." [3] In terms of virtue, then, the condition of the soul's deification is that it respond to God's love so completely that when God sends the Holy Spirit to dwell in the soul, it achieves "a communion, an identification with the Beloved, in which the perfect correspondence of will makes of two, one spirit".[4] As God is Truth, so he is Love. As the soul becomes like Truth by being true, so it becomes like Love through being loving. And as on the side of knowledge the principle on which deification rests is that only like knows like, so on the side of love the principle is that love changes the lover into the beloved.

The principle of love, more specifically than that of truth, indicates how the soul moves toward the restoration of its divine likeness and at what point in its earthly development deification takes place. Love is therefore the subject of the second part of Lady Church's answer, made in response to Will's request to know "By what wey hit wexith" (II:138). First she explains the earthly goal again (II:139-63), but this time as love rather than truth, then the principal means of achieving this goal (II:164-97), finally concluding her sermon, and passus 2, by re-affirming the goal as both truth and love (II:198-205).

The aim of the soul is to know love "kyndely", that is, experimentally, and this takes place through a mutual response between the soul and God. The necessity of a mutual response, in fact, is Lady Church's first answer to the question of "by what wey hit wexith". The truth of this is indicated by the double meaning of the term *love* in Lady Church's discussion, just as there is a double meaning in her use of the term *truth*. When she says:

> Hit is a kynde knowyng . that kenneth in thyn herte
> For to louye thy lord . leuest of alle,
> And deye rathere than to do . eny dedlich synne;
>
> (II:142-44)

the term *love* refers to the love the soul has for God. But when she continues by saying:

---

[3] *Ibid.,* 3.
[4] *Ibid.*

> For treuthe telleth that loue . ys tryacle for synne,
> And most souereyne salue . for saule and for body.
> Loue is the plonte of pees . and most preciouse of
>   vertues;
> For heuene holde hit ne myȝte . so heuy hit semede,
> Til hit hadde on earthe . ȝoten hym-selue;

(II:147-51)

love now refers to God's love for the soul.

This two-sided response is also indicated, and more explicitly, by the first and last statements Lady Church makes in her discussion of the need to know love "kyndely". The first statement, that the heart comes to know naturally that it ought to love God above all things and die rather than do any deadly sin, implies that union with God in love comes about as the result of a free decision and a free turning toward God on the part of the soul, and that the soul can come to this decision and this act by natural means. The freedom of the soul is not only preserved in its relationship with God, but required as well, for man abides in God because he is loved by God, but God abides in man only when God is drawn into the soul by a reciprocal affection.[5] There is in man, therefore, a natural capacity to love God, hence a natural desire to possess him,[6] and a natural inclination to live a perfect moral life in order to be united with God. By his own powers, man can come to the conviction that *"melius est mori quam male uiuere"*. This roots one side of the mystical experience and the Unitive Life in human nature.

Langland is within the bounds of a wide tradition, for the notion that man naturally seeks God was proposed by various medieval theologians, including St. Thomas and St. Bernard.[7]

---

[5]   See St. Bernard, Sermon LXXI, 10, on the *Canticle*.
[6]   "What is it to love God? To wish to possess Him." Hugh of St. Victor, *De Sacramentis*, II, xiii, 6, p. 379.
[7]   Paul Vignaux points out that Ockham, Gabriel Biel, and Duns Scotus all held that man has a natural capacity to love God above all things. See his *Philosophy in the Middle Ages: An Introduction*, trans. by E. C. Hall (New York, 1959), p. 210. St. Thomas also held that man has a natural desire to see God. See Frederick Copleston, *A History of Philosophy* (London, 1950), vol. II, pp. 400-405; and *Sum. Theo.*, I. q. 60, a. 5. For Bernard's full development of this point, see his *De diligendo Deo*, and Gilson's analysis of Bernard's view in *The Spirit of Mediaeval Philosophy*, pp. 289-303, and in *The Mystical Theology of St. Bernard*, pp. 37-42.

Aelred of Rielvaulx expresses the reason for man's natural ability to love God: man was created a rational being, and included in the gift of reason is the ability to love God. This ability, in fact, distinguishes man from lower beings:

And what could be more fitting than that the soul which You created should love You, for this was Your gift to it, that it could love You? For those without reason or sense cannot love You: that is not the nature of their being. Such beings have each their own nature, their own kind, their own order: and though they are not numbered among the blessed and cannot have their being in love of You, they help through their beauty, their goodness, their order towards the glory of those who can be blessed because they can love You.[8]

Ultimately, man can love God because he is created in God's image and likeness. Man is the image of God because he has a free will, according to St. Bernard, and he is like God in being righteous, that is, in being able to desire spiritual things.

The "kynde knowyng" passage from Lady Church's anwer also implies that man has a reason for loving God above all things, for the excercise of the soul's freedom requires knowledge, in this case a "kynde knowyng", which means a knowledge acquired by natural means, and a knowledge that carries such conviction that the whole heart, the affections as well as the intellect, is moved by it. Love of God is natural in the sense of being a natural affection which turns to God as its objects as the result of a knowledge naturally acquired and deeply felt. While the affection itself is innate, it does not turn to God out of a kind of instinct, or even intuition, as Coghill has suggested.[9] As is clear in the passage just quoted from St. Aelred, man by his nature *can* love God, not that he automatically *does* love God. Recognition of God as eminently worthy of love is first required.[10]

---

[8] *The Mirror of Love*, I, i, trans. by Eric Colledge, *The Mediaeval Mystics of England* (New York, 1961), pp. 106-107.

[9] *The Pardon of Piers Plowman*, p. 10.

[10] St. Thomas, *Sum. Theo.*, I-I, q. 60, a. 5, rep. obj. 5, sums up this matter in this way: "Since God's substance and universal goodness are one and the same, all who behold God's essence are by the same movement of love moved towards the Divine essence as it is distinct from other things, and according as it is the universal Good. And because He is naturally loved by all so far as He is the universal good, it is impossible that whoever sees Him in His essence should not love Him. But such as do not

Langland agrees with Hilton, who says, "love follows knowledge and not the other way about".[11]

What this "kynde knowyng" involves is explained by Lady Church in the rest of her discussion on the principle of love. The purpose of this passage, in fact, is not only to explain what happens when the soul unites itself to God, but also to convince Will that he ought to love God:

> For treuthe telleth that loue . ys tryacle for synne,
> And most souereyne salue . for saule and for body.
> Loue is the plonte of pees . and most preciouse of vertues;
> For heuene holde hit ne my3te . so heuy hit semede,
> Till hit hadde on erthe . 3oten hym-selue.
> Was neuere lef vp-on lynde . lyghter ther-after,
> As whanne hit hadde of the folde . flesch and blod ytake;
> Tho was it portatyf and pershaunt . as the point of a nelde,
> May non armure hit lette . nother hye walles;
> For-thy is loue ledere . of oure lordes folke in heuene,
> And a mene, as the meyere is . by-twyne the kygn and
> the comune,
> Ry3t so is loue a ledere . and the law shapeth;
> Up man for hus mysdedes . the mercement he taxeth.

(II:147-59)

The overall reason here is love itself, meaning, now, divine Love. When the soul comes to a heartfelt knowledge of the nature of Love, Lady Church says, in effect, it will naturally desire Love above all things and rather die than put obstacles in the way of its possession. The first point she makes about the nature of Love is that it is "tryacle for synne" and "soueryne salue . for saule and for body". This statement sums up the whole doctrine of justification of the ungodly. As the result of the Fall, the interior man is in a state of disorder; that is, his mind is no longer subservient to God and the inferior powers of his soul are no longer subservient to the superior powers. Such a man is "ungodly", in a state of sin, and unable to overcome the infirmities of mind and

---

behold His essence, know Him by some particular effects, which are sometimes opposed to their will. So in this way they are said to hate God; yet nevertheless, so far as He is the universal good of all, every thing naturally loves God more than itself."

[11] *Scale*, II, 34, p. 247.

body included in the punishment of the Fall. The "ungodly" soul is justified through the infusion of grace and the remission of sins.[12] This work, Walter Hilton explains, is especially the work of Love and appropriated to the Holy Spirit. The Creation of the soul belongs to the Father because it manifests God's power; the Redemption belongs to the Son because it manifests God's wisdom; [13] "but the justification and salvation of a soul by the forgiveness of sins is appropriated to the Third Person, that is, to the Holy Ghost. For it is in our justification that God most shows His love for us, and it is that which most demands our love in return." Hilton emphasizes the greatness of God's act by explaining that while Creation is common to all creatures, Redemption common to all souls, including those who are not willing to profit by it, "the justification and sanctification of our souls through the gift of the Holy Ghost is the work only of Love, and that is not common to all, but is a special gift to the elect, and is the special work of love for us who are His chosen children". This love, Hilton concludes, the soul ought to desire, "for this love is God Himself, the Holy Ghost".[14] Thus, when the soul sees that Love is its justification, it naturally desires it.

The soul will desire Love through also becoming aware that Love is the plant of peace and the most precious of virtues. The description of love as the "plonte of pees" has a theological accuracy, for peace is one of the effects or "fruits" of love.[15] Peace means the simultaneous possession of a twofold concord: an external concord and an internal. External concord is that between the individual and other men, "in so far as the wills of various hearts agree together in consenting to the same thing",[16] and is the fruit of fraternal love, the second precept of the law of charity. It is also concord between the individual and God,

[12] See *Sum. Theo.,* I-II, q. 113; and II-II, q. 23, a. 2, rep. obj. 3.
[13] "For He overcame the devil principally through His wisdom and not through strength", which is exactly how Langland dramatizes the Redemption in the *Vita,* XXI:271-451.
[14] *Scale,* II, 34, pp. 250-251.
[15] The interior effects of love are joy, peace, and mercy; the exterior effects are beneficence, almsdeeds, and fraternal correction. See *Sum. Theo.,* II-II, qq. 28-33.
[16] *Ibid.,* II-II, q. 29, a. 1.

again insofar as the individual's will and God's will agree in consenting to the same thing, and is the fruit of a mutual love between
God and man, the first precept of the law of charity.[17] But there
must also be internal concord if there is to be peace, and this
is the "tranquility of order"[18] that the individual enjoys when
all his appetitive movements agree in tending toward the same
object. Thus peace is directly tied to justification, for internal
order is enjoyed only by the justified soul whose sins have been
remitted, and "sin is remitted to us, when God is at peace with
us, and this peace consists in the love whereby God loves us".[19]
It is the gift of Love, with its effects of justification and peace,
that enables Free Choice to rule "sweetly" as well as
"mightily".

Complete harmony of life is realized perfectly, to the extent
possible on earth, with the experiencing of contemplation and
entrance into the Unitive Life. The perfect Christian achieves
such purity and is so united with God that not only are his soul's
powers set in order, but he enjoys the intimate harmony of all
virtues, even those, such as fortitude and meekness, wisdom and
prudence, justice and mercy, which seem opposed.[20] He also lives
harmoniously with God and men to an eminent degree, for his
soul has not only become the permanent habitation of the Holy
Spirit, but he becomes God's co-worker in the salvation of men's
souls. And all this because the sanctified soul, abiding in God
and God in it, is guided by charity alone. There is a progressive
simplification in the life of the spirit, with all virtuous concerns
and spiritual anxieties moving toward, and finally becoming
dissolved in, the single fact of charity.

That love is the "most preciouse of vertues" is obvious, since
salvation is not possible without charity, and the rewards of love
just described are eminently desirable. This phrase sums up the
value of love for the soul, and what follows in the same sentence
explains whence the value of love ultimately derives. "For heuene

---

[17]   *Ibid.*, a. 3.
[18]   *Ibid.*, a. 1, rep. obj. 1.
[19]   *Ibid.*, I-II, q. 113, a. 2.
[20]   Garrigou-Lagrange, *op. cit.*, p. 178. Also *Sum. Theo.*, II-II, q. 81, a. 8.

holde hit ne myȝte", Lady Church says, until it had taken on flesh and blood and delivered itself to its creatures. Again we may note the theological accuracy of this poetic expression, since it is of the very nature of charity, which "seeketh not her own" (I Cor. xiii, 5), to communicate itself, be it charity in God or in man.[21] But the point made here is that love is the soul's consolation and the most precious of virtues because it comes from God. As truth derives its value from being like Truth, so love derives its value from coming from Love.

The last point made in this passage is that not only is love the leader of the soul to God, in the sense of being the mediary, the point of contact, between God and man, but it also shapes the law, exacting from man payment for his misdeeds. In this way also does love lead the soul to God. As Lady Church stated at the beginning of this passage, the soul naturally loves God when it knows the nature of God as Love, and naturally desires to live the moral life necessary to be united with God. Like truth, love is not only the soul's end, but also its means; at once the object for which and the rule of conduct by which the soul lives. When man's will conforms to God's will, in other words, it makes God's will its own law.

Having explained that the soul naturally embraces Love when it comes to know the nature of Love and the rewards it offers the soul, Lady Church concludes her discussion of "by what wey hit wexith" by explaining the reciprocal response God makes to the soul:

> And for to knowe it kyndeliche . his comseth by myghte,
> In the herte, there is the hefd . and the hye welle.
> Of kynde knowyng in herte . ther comseth a myghte,
> That falleth to the fader . that formede ous alle.
>
> (II:160-63)

Union with God in love is complete, therefore, when God the Father sends the Holy Spirit, who is Love, into the soul that has made a free response to God's love. This roots the other side of the mystical experience in the divine nature and makes it essentially a supernatural experience. The soul may prepare itself

[21] See St. Bernard, *On the Necessity of Loving God,* XII, pp. 260-63.

for mystical union, but union does not finally come about except by God's act. The result is the soul's feeling a power in its heart which it recognizes as coming from God: that is, the soul is consciously aware, has a "kynde knowyng", of the Holy Spirit dwelling in it. Such an experience is none other than contemplation, and is the point at which the soul is deified. To be consciously aware of the indwelling of the Holy Spirtit in one's heart requires the higher degrees of sanctifying grace and is therefore not possible to the ordinary Christian, who receives only the lower degrees of this grace. To achieve conscious union with God is to achieve the Unitive Life, the life in which the will is fully in accord with God's will, the natural likeness to God is restored, and the soul passes into the service of God; the life, in short, of the soul deified by the fulness of grace. The difference between the ordinary Christian and the perfect Christian is that the former knows and believes that sanctifying grace unites man to God imperfectly in this life and perfectly in the next, while the latter achieves an experimental knowledge of God dwelling in him. The soul in the ordinary state of grace accepts by faith the truth of deification; the perfect soul actually realizes deification in this life.

Many modern theologians agree on this point,[22] and Walter Hilton made this clear in Langland's day. He explained that a conscious awareness of the life of grace is possible only to the perfect; that though infrequently achieved, it is nevertheless in the normal way of sanctifying grace; and that such an awareness is none other than mystical contemplation. His entire teaching on this matter is summarized in the following passage:

While a soul is overlaid and blinded by the love of the world it is entirely extraverted. It lies open to everything like a highway, for every impulse of the flesh or the devil makes itself felt. But then by grace the soul is withdrawn into a secret chamber where it sees God and hears His secret counsels, and it is wonderfully consoled ... This tasting of manna is an awareness of the life of grace, which comes from the opening of the soul's eyes. And this grace does not

[22]   This is the entire thesis of Garrigou-Lagrange, *op. cit.*, who develops it on the basis of St. Thomas's teaching. For a brief statement of this matter, see Pascal Parente, *The Mystical Life*, pp. 163-69.

differ from the grace that an elect soul feels at the beginning of its conversion; it is the same grace but experienced in another way, because the progress of the soul and grace are interdependent. The purer and more detached from the love of the world the soul is, the stronger is the grace, the more interior and spiritual the experience of the presence of God. So the same grace that first turns men from sin and then makes them set out and advance on the spiritual road by the practice of virtues and good works makes them perfect, and it is called an *awareness of the life of grace,* for he who has it is conscious of the grace within him ... The more that the eyes are shut to the things of earth in this sort of sleep, the clearer is the inward vision which loving contemplation brings of the beauty of heaven. Love brings about this sleep and this waking in the soul of the lover of God through the light of grace.[23]

And lest we imagine that Hilton's passage does not apply to what Lady Church says, because Hilton speaks of experiencing grace while Lady Church speaks of experiencing Love, we should recall one point that Hilton takes pains to make:

Perhaps you wonder why I say at one time that grace performs all this, at another time Love, or Jesus, or God. I reply that when I say that grace does it I mean love, Jesus, God; they are all the same. Jesus is Love, Jesus is grace, Jesus is God; for He does everything in us by grace, as God, and for Love. For this reason I can use which word of the four I please in this book.[24]

Contemplation is the awareness of Love, the Holy Spirit, dwelling in the soul; but contemplation is also the point at which the soul is deified. Again we may refer to Hilton, who says that "true contemplation ... makes the soul conform to God",[25] and who distinguishes the third degree of contemplation from the two lesser degrees in terms of the soul's conformity to the Trinity:

The third degree of contemplation – which is the highest that can be reached in this life – consists of both knowledge and love; in knowing God and the perfect love of Him. And that comes about when a man, first of all reformed in the image of Jesus by the practice of virtue, then visited by grace, is detached from all earthly and carnal love, from useless thoughts and imaginations, and is carried out of his bodily senses. By the grace of the Holy Ghost his intellect

[23]   *Scale,* II, 40, pp. 276-79.
[24]   *Ibid.,* 42, p. 292.
[25]   *Ibid.,* I, 14, p. 20.

is illuminated to see Truth itself, which is God, and spiritual matters, and his will is inflamed with a soft, sweet, burning love. So powerfully does this come about that by an ecstasy of love the soul for the time being becomes one with God and is conformed to the image of the Trinity. The beginning of this contemplation may be felt in this life, but the fullness of it is kept for the bliss of heaven. Of this union with our Lord St. Paul says: *Qui adhaeret Deo unus spiritus est cum illo* (I Cor. vi. 17). Whoever in ecstasy of love is joined to God, then God and his soul are not two but one. And in truth in this union a marriage is made between God and the soul, which shall never be broken.[26]

Hilton's statement parallels in thought the teaching of St. Bernard, who also held that man's divine similitude is fully restored, as far as possible in this life, at the moment of contemplation:

Assuredly it is a likeness wonderful and admirable, which accompanies the vision of God, or, rather, it is that vision itself. For I understand this of the vision which is brought about by love, for in love is that vision and that likeness. Who does not stand amazed at the great love of God in recalling to Himself a soul by which He has been scorned? It is with justice, then, that that wicked one, who was represented in a former sermon as usurping to himself the likeness of God, is severely censured, since in loving iniquity he is not able to love either himself or God, as it is written: *He that loveth iniquity hateth his own soul* (Ps. x. 6, Douay). The iniquity, then, which is in part the cause of the unlikeness between God and the soul, being taken out of the way, there shall be between them a spiritual union perfect and entire, a mutual discernment and vision, a reciprocal love. *When that which is perfect is come, then that which is in part shall be done away*, and there shall be between God and the soul a perfect and consummated affection, a full knowledge, a vision manifest, a firm union, an indivisible society, a perfect similitude. Then the soul shall *know, even as also it is known* (I Cor. xiii. 10, 12); then shall it love even as it is loved, and the Bridegroom shall rejoice over the Bride, because knowledge and love are reciprocal between them.[27]

God is possessed, then, according to Lady Church, by the soul who, loving God, is united by God with Love itself, the Holy Spirit, and knows God experimentally. Union in love is a union

[26]   *Ibid.*, I, 8, pp. 11-12.
[27]   Sermon LXXXII, 8 on the *Canticle*.

of wills, for as St. Thomas says, "love is naturally the first act of the will and appetite; for which reason all the other appetite movements presuppose love as their root and origin".[28] Indeed, the very possibility of union with God in love rests on the fact that both God and man have a will: "in whomsoever there is will and appetite, there must also be love: since if the first is wanting, all that follows is also wanting. Now it has been shown that will is in God (Q. 19, A. 1), and hence we must attribute love to him." [29] Love is the point of contact between God and man, and this, again, is the sense in which Lady Church says:

> For-thy is loue ledere . of our lordes folke in heuene,
> And a mene, as the meyere is . by-twyne the king and
>   the comune,
> Ryȝt so is loue a ledere ... (II:156-58)

Herein lies the connection between the two parts of Lady Church's sermon: truth is to be like Truth through a conformity of wills; love unites man to Love, also through a conformity of wills. The fruit is mutual knowledge and love between God and man, which is contemplation and the unitive life.

After explaining the nature of the goal and what happens when it is achieved, Lady Church then discusses the principal virtues, the means, by which the end is achieved (II:164-99). The two virtues are simply humility (meekness) and active charity. Humility has the broad sense of including everything contrary to self-love; active charity, or fraternal charity, has the broad sense of good works toward one's neighbor. By the first, God is loved more than self, and his will is placed above self-will; by the second, one's neighbor is loved as oneself. These two virtues are commonly emphasized by mystics. Hilton names them as the virtues which principally conform the soul to God:

turn both internally and externally to God, and conform yourself inwardly to His likeness by humility and charity and the other virtues, and so you will be truly converted to Him.[30]

---

[28] *Sum. Theo.,* I-I, q. 20, a. 1.
[29] *Ibid.*
[30] *Scale,* I, 1, p. 3.

He further describes these two virtues as being the "special livery of Jesus" and those necessary for contemplation:

As long as He does not find His image reformed in you He is a stranger and far removed from you. Strive therefore to be arrayed in His likeness, that is in humility and charity, which form His livery, and then He will know you intimately and show you His secrets. . . . No virtue or work that you may do will make you like our Lord without humility and charity, for these two are specially God's livery. If you will be like Him, have humility and charity.[31]

Richard Rolle, answering the question, "How sal I verrayli lufe God?" also joins humility to charity, for the Holy Ghost dwells in the meek soul:

þe thirde askyng es: How sal I verrayli lufe God? I answer: Verray lufe es, to lufe hym in al þi sawle devowtely and swetely. Stalwortly may na man lufe hym, bot he be stalworth. He es stalworth, þat es meke; for al gastly strengh comes of mekenes, on whame restes þe Haly Gaste in a meke sawle.[32]

The author of *The Cloud of Unknowing*, finally, gives us the reason for singling out humility and charity: because these two contain all virtues. Incidentally, he also gives us the definition of virtue that is identical with that of St. Bernard, Richard of St. Victor, Rolle, and Hilton, and that is applicable to Langland's use of the term:

For vertewe is no elles bot an ordeinde & a mesurid affeccion, pleinly directe vnto God for him-self. For whi he in him-self is þe clene cause of alle vertewes; in so mochel þat 3if any man be sterid to any o vertewe by any oþer cause medelid wiþ him – 3e, þof al it be þe cheef – 3it þat vertewe is þan inparfite. As þus, bi ensaumple, may be seen in o vertewe or two in stede of all þe oþer. & wel may þeese two vertewes be meeknes & / charite, for who-so mi3t gete þeese two cleerly, him nedid no mo: for whi he had alle.[33]

Such is the nature of union with God in love and the principal virtues by which the soul is prepared for it. While this union is essentially a supernatural experience, resting, finally, in God's

---

[31]   *Ibid.*, I, 51, p. 81.
[32]   *The Form of Living*, X, 11. 99-105, in *English Writings of Richard Rolle*, ed. by Hope Emily Allen (Oxford, 1931), p. 111.
[33]   Phyllis Hodgson's edition, *op. cit.*, XII, 11. 17-24, p. 39.

will alone, God does not send the Holy Spirit into the heart unless the individual turns to God's love freely and out of his own conviction. Lady Church's claim that man naturally knows he ought to love God is important, because it means that love of God is already in the heart but is not aware of itself. "If the love of God were not already within us", writes Gilson, "we should never succeed in putting it there for ourselves". The essential problem, he continues, "is not how to acquire the love of God, but rather how to make it fully aware of itself, of its object, and of the way it should bear itself towards this object. In this sense we might say that the only difficulty is that of education, or, if you prefer it, the re-education of love." [34] This statement accurately describes the difficulty Will faces and overcomes in the course of this poem, and explains why the drama of *Piers Plowman* centers on Will's quest for education. Will seeks education in love, in the sense of his already impelling love of God becoming progressively aware of itself until it dominates all other affections and concerns and becomes his life. He seeks to know God experimentally, by feeling as well as by faith. Instruction in theological matters and moral problems is not his goal, but is the preparation and the approach to the wisdom he seeks to "know kyndely". "Instruction", St. Bernard says, "renders men learned, but feeling makes them wise ... The former, then, gives a certain approach, as it were, to wisdom, but the latter an entrance into it".[35] Or, to quote from the Middle English treatise on "Propyr wille", charity, the common will,

is swa parfyte þat alle þe wytte of þis werlde can nouʒt teche it: for qwy, gastly wytte and vndyrstandynge is tauʒte of god by felyng, and naman may make a feler in gastly wytte bot god þat is þe gyfer. Þe techyng of god is gyfen, and þat gyfynge causyth felynge. And in þis felynge is fully knawen þe difference of þase men þat ere tauʒte of god – as þase þat gyfe þam to parfyte lyuynge, and þase þat er tauʒt of men – as þase þat gyfe þam to comyn lyfe.[36]

---

[34] *Spirit of Mediaeval Philosophy,* pp. 279-80.
[35] Sermon XXIII, 14, on the *Canticle.*
[36] *Op. cit.,* pp. 173-74.

VII. *DEUS CARITAS* AND TRUTH

That *Piers Plowman* is governed by this essentially mystical scheme of salvation is supported by the *Deus caritas* text, which sanctions Lady Church's teaching, and by Piers's description of the Highway to Truth. How the *Deus caritas* text supports Lady Church's sermon has not yet been considered. But now that the basic ideas contained in the doctrine of deification have been brought forward, this problem can be examined efficiently.[1]

The *Deus caritas* text from St. John's epistle is of fundamental importance to mystics, especially those who distil the union between the soul and God to a union in charity, who give importance to man's loving faculty as well as his knowing faculty, and who emphasize the restoration of the soul's divine likeness as necessary for salvation. The first of the two verses in which the

---

[1] Despite the importance Lady Church gives to the *Deus caritas* text as providing the scriptural basis of all she says about the way of salvation, scholars have largely ignored the relationship between this text and her sermon. Among the few who have touched on this problem is Father Dunning, *Interpretation of the A-text,* pp. 42-44. But Dunning considers relevant only four verses from the introductory part of St. John's epistle (Verses 4-8) in which St. John admonishes his audience not to listen to false teachers, and concludes that Lady Church is opposing the spirit of truth to the spirit of error. Dunning's discussion is inadequate for several reasons: (1) it ignores the fact that this text governs the entire answer Lady Church gives to Will, for she recalls it at the end of her sermon as well as the beginning; (2) the actual words *Deus caritas* do not figure in the part of St. John's epistle which Dunning considers relevant; (3) and St. John's warning against false teachers serves only to prepare his audience for what he is about to say, so that the remaining fourteen verses carry the really important part of John's message. Robertson and Huppé also pause over the *Deus caritas* text, but only in two footnotes (*op. cit.,* pp. 42-43, notes 49 and 50) and their discussion is obscure.

actual words "God is love" appear is: "He who does not love does not love does not know God; for God is love" (I John iv, 8). In this text, Gilson points out in his study of St. Bernard,

we have the source of the doctrine, afterwards so famous, of charity as knowledge, or even as vision, of God. The least that can be said is that such a text supposes that the man who has nothing in himself of what God is in essence is incapable of knowing God. St. Bernard himself adds practically nothing to the text, indeed I believe he adds absolutely nothing, for he contents himself with merely making it more precisely clear that the "likeness" of man to God is the condition of our knowledge of God, and that this likeness is the work of charity.[2]

The other passage is: "God is love, and who abides in love abides in God, and God in him" (I John iv, 16). For the implications of this passage we can go directly to St. Bernard.

And yet we think that God and man abide each mutually in the other, but in a manner far different from that just referred to [concerning the unity of the Trinity], because their substances and their wills are distinct, and they abide each in the other in a manner far different; that is, they are not blended as to substances, but consentaneous as to wills. And this union is to them a communion of wills and a conformity in charity.[3]

The very kernel of the doctrine of deification, of man's salvation through being like God in a conformity of wills, thereby achieving earthly union with God in love, arises out of a close but literal understanding of the *Deus caritas* verses. Langland must have had the immediate implications of these verses in mind and expected his readers to be equally knowledgeable. They explain why Lady Church can say that in order to be saved one must be true, that truth consists in the alignment of man's will with God's so that in word, thought, and deed he does what God wills be done, that in being true a man is like God, that one grows in truth by growing in love, and the culmination of this growth is to have a "kynde knowyng" of God abiding in one's own heart, and that all of this teaching is based on the *Deus caritas* text. Lady Church's sermon is a practical working out of the principle that

[2]   *The Mystical Theology of St. Bernard,* p. 22.
[3]   Sermon LXXI, 10, on the *Canticle.*

since God is Love, man must be loving, and thus like God, if he is to know God.

The *Deus caritas* text also explains the twofold use of the term *truth* to describe God's will as the right rule of action and man's will as right if it corresponds to God's will. It explains, furthermore, the interchangeability of *truth* and *love*. As Langland uses these terms, they may be substituted in St. John's statement so that "who does not love does not know God, for God is love" may very well read "who is not true does not know God, for God is truth". Interchanging these terms is possible because both describe those attributes in God which can, and must, be realized in man, according to the principle that if one wishes to be saved, one must be like God.

These verses also explain, finally, why the Dreamer seeks to know "kyndely", refusing to rest until his desire for a "kynde knowyng" of spiritual matters, and ultimately God, is satisfied. The knowledge St. John speaks of, and that mystics desire, is not an objective, reasoned knowledge, but an immediate awareness, a degree of experiential knowledge achievable only when the soul is really united with God in love. To know God, abide in God, love God, be united with God, all are the same thing in St. John's teaching, and in Lady Church's as well. The peculiar inquisitiveness Langland gives Will is not an arbitrarily assigned characteristic nor dictated merely by dramatic necessity; it is determined by the doctrine of deification, or rather by the fact that in *Piers Plowman* Langland develops the way of salvation as inferred from St. John's epistle. Will seeks to know God through a mutual abiding, through a conscious awareness of the life of grace, through seeing "Treuthe sytte . in they selue herte" (VIII:255).

St. John's epistle is not only the scriptural basis for the idea of salvation through becoming like God, but also the source of Lady Church's explanation of "by what wey hit wexith". Her first response to this question from Will is to say that one knows naturally that God must be loved above all things. This sort of reply indicates that Will's question asks not only in what way one grows towards likeness with God, but also how and why one comes to love God. In other words, Will's question covers three problems involved in the principle of love: (1) the way in which man is united with God in love; (2) how it is possible for man to love God; and (3) what the reason is for man's loving God. Lady Church, like St. John, deals with all three problems simultaneously, but let us take them one by one.

The way in which man is united to God in love is explained by St. John when he says not only that "God is love", but also that "love is from God" (Verse 7) and that this love which comes from God is the Holy Spirit: "In this we know that we abide in him and he in us, because he has given us of his Spirit" (Verse 13). This means there is the Charity which is God, the charity which comes to man as a gift from God, and the Holy Spirit which is identified with the gift of charity and is therefore the bond which unites the soul to God. Thus the soul is united to God in love through God's giving himself to the soul by sending the Holy Spirit to dwell in it. Here is the basis in the *Deus caritas* text for Lady Church's saying:

> And for to knowe it kyndelich . hit comseth by myghte,
> In the herte, ther is the hefd . and the hye welle.
> Of kynde knowyng in herte . ther comseth a myghte,
> That falleth to the fader . that formede ous alle.

> (II:160-65)

This understanding of St. John is found in both Bernard and Hilton. We may again refer to Gilson's work for a summary of Bernard's position.

If God is charity, and if charity must needs be in us if we are to know God, then charity must of necessity be given by God. There we have the origin of the distinction, so important in St. Bernard, between the Charity which is God, and the charity which in us is the "gift" of God. This distinction is suggested by the verse that declares that charity comes from God: "Caritas ex Deo est" (I *John*, IV, 7).

A new thesis, not less important, is added to the foregoing by the identification of the gift of charity with the gift of the Holy Spirit. That is a point which the Cistercian mystics always had in mind; it explains why the Holy Spirit always, in their doctrine, plays the part of the bond by which the soul is united to God and the spiritual life becomes a participation in the Divine life: "In hoc cognoscimus quoniam in eo manemus, et ipse in nobis, quoniam *de Spiritu suo* dedit nobis" (I *John*, IV, 13)[4]

In order to explain why he exhorts his pupil to desire nothing but the love of God, even though the soul's happiness and end lies in the knowledge of God, Walter Hilton also explicates St. John's text in a way that is essentially identical to St. Bernard's, yet relates these ideas to contemplation and the reformation of the soul's divine likeness. Hilton's entire chapter (chap. 34 of Book II) is pertinent to our present problem, but I shall quote two passages only.

The saints say, and rightly, that there are two sorts of spiritual love. One is called uncreated and the other created. Uncreated Love is God Himself the Third Person of the Trinity, that is the Holy Ghost. He is uncreated Love; as St. John says: *Deus dilectio est* (I John iv. 8). God is love, that is the Holy Ghost. Created love is the love that the Holy Ghost arouses in a soul at the sight of truth, that is of God. This love is called created because it is brought about by the Holy Ghost. Being created it is not God Himself, but it is the love which the soul feels at the contemplation of God, when it is drawn to Him alone. Now you can see how created love is not the cause of a soul coming to the contemplation of God. For there are some who think that they can love God so ardently, as it were by their own powers, that they can merit the contemplation of Him, but it is not so. It is uncreated Love, that is God Himself, who is the cause of all this knowledge. For owing to sin and the weakness of its nature the poor, blind soul is so far from the clear knowledge of God and the enjoyment of His love that it would never be able to attain them, if it were not for the infinite greatness of God's love. But because He loves us so much, He gives us His love, that is the Holy Ghost. He is both the giver and the gift, and by that gift makes us know and love Him. This is the love that I said you should desire, this uncreated Love that is the Holy Ghost. And indeed a lesser gift than He will not avail to bring us to the blessed knowledge of God. Therefore we should desire and ask of God only this gift of Love; that in the greatness of His blessed love He would illumine our hearts with His incomprehensible light that we may know Him, and that He may impart His blessed love to us, that as He loves us, so we may love Him in return.[5]

---

[4] *The Mystical Theology of Saint Bernard,* pp. 22-23.
[5] *Scale,* II, 34, pp. 248-49.

This love is nothing else than God Himself, who does all this in a man's soul by love, and reforms it in feeling to His likeness ... This love brings the fullness of virtues into the soul, virtues which are pure and true, gentle and easy, and it makes their performance a matter of love and pleasure ... This love elevates the soul from a carnal to a spiritual state, from being immersed in the things of earth to enjoying those of heaven, from the vain consideration of earthly things to the contemplation of the spiritual world and the secrets of God.[6]

Although union with God is brought about by God's love for the soul, the soul must meet the conditions which prepare it for the indwelling of the Holy Spirit. According to St. John, the condition set for man is that he respond to God's love by performing acts of fraternal charity. Each man who loves God does God's will, and God's will is that each man actively love his fellow men:

Beloved, let us love one another, for love is from God.   (Verse 7)

If we love one another, God abides in us and his love is perfected in us.

(Verse 12)

If anyone says, "I love God," and hates his brother, he is a liar. For how can he who does not love his brother, whom he sees, love God, whom he does not see? And this commandment we have from him, that he who loves God should love his brother also.

(Verses 20-21)

Thus, after first explaining that the soul knows love "kyndeliche" when the Holy Ghost comes to man's heart, Lady Church devotes most of the long middle part of her sermon on "by what wey hit wexith" (II:169-99) to the necessity of fraternal charity. As is consistent with her practice, and with Langland's reformist intention, she applies the second precept of the law of charity to specific cases, particularly to the obligation of almsgiving to the poor, but she nevertheless emphasizes the principle itself of active charity as the basis of merit:

> Thauh ȝe be trewe of ȝoure tonge . and trewelich wynne,
> And be as chast as a chyld . that nother chit ne fyghteth,
> Bote yf ȝe loue leellichte . and lene the poure,
> Of such good as god sent . goodliche parte,

[6] *Ibid.,* p. 252.

ʒe haue no more meryt . in masse ne in houres,
Than Malkyn of hure maidenhod . wham no man desireth.
　　For Iamys the gentel . iuggeth in hus bokes,
That feith with-oute fet . ys febelere than nouht,
And ded as a dore nayle . bote yf the dede folwe;
　　　　Fides sine operibus mortua est.
Chastite with-oute charite . worth cheynid in helle;
Hit is as lewede as a lampe . that no lyght ys ynne.　(II:176-86)

The need to give alms in particular, and to observe the commandment of active charity in general, is incumbent on all Christians,
the imperfect and the perfect alike. In making this elementary
(because fundamentally Christian) point, Lady Church has not
abandoned the higher level of her spiritual teaching and descended
to the level of mere catechism, for the observance of active
charity is necessary for the restoration of man's divine similitude,
the achieving of contemplation, and the final transformation by
which man is fully deified. St. Bernard is careful to make this
point when he discusses man's uprightness, his desire for spiritual
things, as one of the elements of similitude between God and
man. He first explains where this divine similitude is located in
man, and the need to restore it in order to behold "as in a glass
the glory of the Lord" and to be "changed into the same image"
of the Lord by the Holy Ghost:

Therefore God 'made man upright' according to the mind, not according to the earth and material body. For He created him in His
own image and similitude (Gen. i. 27) ... God, then, who is upright,
made man upright and similar to Himself, that is to say, without
unrighteousness, even as there is no unrighteousness in Him. Now,
unrighteousness is a vice of the heart, not of the flesh, and from this
you know that the likeness of God which you have is to be preserved, or to be restored, in the spiritual part of your nature, and not
in its earthy and clayey part. For God is Spirit, and it behoves those
who desire to become like Him, or to persevere in His likeness, to
enter into their heart, and to employ themselves in the spirit in that
blessed work; so that with open face, beholding as in a glass the
glory of the Lord, they may be changed into the same image from
glory to glory, even as by the Spirit of the Lord (2 Cor. iii. 18).[7]

---

[7]　Sermon XXIV, 5, on the *Canticle*. Note that contemplation and deification are the work of the Holy Spirit, and that this point is based on St.
Paul as well as on St. John.

Then he repeats the definition of rectitude and explains the need for active charity "in order that this rectitude may be perfect":

Therefore, to seek and to have a love for things which are on the earth is to bend down and deform the soul; while, on the contrary, to think of, and to long for, the things which are above is its uprightness. And in order that this rectitude may be perfect, it must exist first in the mind, and then pass into the life (*in sensu et consensu*). I should, in fact, call you upright if you think aright in all things, and your actions accord with your thoughts. Let your faith and your actions declare the condition of your mind, which is invisible. Consider as upright him whom you have ascertained to be Catholic in faith and righteous in actions. If one of these two be wanting, do not hesitate to conclude that he is deficient in uprightness; for you have in the Scripture: *If thou offerest rightly, but dost not rightly divide, thou hast sinned* (Gen. iv. 7). Whichsoever, indeed, of these two, faith and works, you offer to God, you do rightly; but you do not rightly to divide either from the other. Since you are right in offering, be not wrong in dividing. Why do you divide works from faith? Wrongly are you dividing, and the division destroys your faith; for *faith without works is dead* (James ii. 20).[8]

In this way the *Deus caritas* text not only gives rise to Lady Church's discussion of the way of the soul's union with God, but also makes clear the coherence of her discussion. The soul is in the way of love when it responds to God's love, preferring death to sin, observing the law of love through performing acts of charity. Its reward is the experience of contemplation, a conscious awareness of the indwelling of the Holy Spirit, felt as a power coming from the Father. At this point the soul achieves "truth" and has a good hope of salvation because it bears a likeness to God. St. John sums up the way of love when he says:

In this is love perfected with us, that we may have confidence in the day of judgment; because as he is, even so are we also in this world.
(Verse 17)

The second problem involved in the principle of love, how it is possible for men to love God, is already solved by the soul's love coming as a gift from God. The soul is able to love God "because God first loved us" (Verse 19). The proof of this is the Incarnation, the act of divine love which made the gift of love available

[8] *Ibid.*, paragraph 7.

to man and redeemed him so that he is capable of receiving this gift. St. John insists on this point:

In this has the love of God been shown in our case, that God has sent his only-begotten Son into the World that we may live through him. In this is the love, not that we have loved God, but that he has first loved us, and sent his Son a propitiation for our sins.

(Verses 9-10)

And we have seen, and do testify, that the Father has sent his Son to be Savior of the world.

(Verse 14)

And Lady Church also insists on it:

For heuene holde hit ne myʒte . so heuy hit semede,
Til hit hadde on erthe . ʒoten hym-selue.
Was neuere lef vp-on lynde . lyghter ther-after,
As whanne hit hadde of the folde . flesch and blod ytake;
Tho was it portatyf and pershaunt . as the poynt of a nelde,
May non armure hit lette . nother hye walles;
For-thy is loue ledere . of oure lordes folke if heuene,
And a mene, as the meyere is . bytwyne the king and the
    commune,
Ryʒt so is loue a ledere . . .   (II:150-58)

On ous he lokyde with loue . and let hus sone deye,
Meekliche for oure mysdedes . to amendy ous alle.

(II:164-65)

The reason for man's loving God, finally, is also inherent in love's both coming from God and being God. Lady Church says that once the soul knows the nature of love it will naturally desire to possess it and to live by its law, and she roots the value of love in the fact that it comes from God. This is the point St. John makes in his opening statement, "Beloved, let us love one another, for love is from God" (Verse 7). One's neighbor should be loved not for the neighbor's sake, but for love's sake, and love should be desired because it comes from God and is God. And when Lady Church draws the conclusion that love is therefore the leader of our Lord's folk in heaven, she makes essentially the same point John makes in the very next verse: "And everyone who loves is born of God, and knows God" (Verse 8).

The *Deus caritas* epistle is thus both a scriptural basis for the doctrine of deification and the basis of Lady Church's sermon. And Lady Church's sermon, in turn, lays the theological foundation on which *Piers Plowman* is built. Piers's Highway to Truth is also an answer to the question of how one saves his soul, and also reveals the theological foundations of Langland's poem. Piers's teaching has a different character from Lady Church's, but both mark out the same goal and the same essential means. In keeping with her role as *Magistra*, Lady Church deals only with basic theological principles governing the way of perfection; in keeping with his role as God's humble co-worker in the salvation of men's souls, Piers deals with the more particular moral steps leading the soul to union with Truth. Piers's teaching is more detailed than Lady Church's because he is dealing with the soul who has already made some progress toward truth, rather than with the soul who has not yet begun the way. In the Meed episode, having resolved to be free of the inferior appetites which deform the soul and pervert its desire for peace, the soul has turned its mind to Truth. In the confessions, aroused by fear of God's punishment for sins to a resolution to sin no more, the soul has turned its heart to Truth as well. Nevertheless, its conversion thus far has been fragile and its desire for Truth impatient. It barely begins to move forward when it "blostered forth as bestes . over baches and hulles" (VIII:159): that is, it finds itself still vulnerable to temptation and blocked by ignorance. It is up to Piers, now, to instruct the soul and encourage it to persevere. His instruction strengthens its patience by enabling it to foresee the labour of the way, and its desire by showing it the final reward. The frightened soul may then refuse the undertaking, but the encouraged soul will make a second and more lasting effort of subduing its bodily appetites by working in Piers's half-acre. In this way, the Highway to Truth answers the question of salvation in a way that responds to the specific need of the soul at a certain point in its progress.

Piers's Highway, however, leads to the same goal marked out by Lady Church, and develops the same principal means. The goal is actually to see Truth dwelling in one's heart:

> And yf Grace graunte the . to go yn in thys wise,
> Thow shalt see Treuthe sytte . in thy selue herte,
> And solace thy soule . saue the fro pyne.
> Al-so charge Charyte . a churche to make
> In thyn hole herte . to herberghwen alle treuthe,
> And fynde alle manere folke . fode to hure saules,
> Yf loue and leaute . and owre lawe be trewe:
>> *Quodcumque petieritis in nomine meo, dabitur*
>> *enim vobis.*

(VIII:254-60)

Actually to see Truth can only mean to achieve comtemplation, the conscious awareness of the indwelling of the Holy Spirit.[9] To find solace of soul and salvation from pain is to find the peace that is the fruit of love and the perfect justification which remits all sin. To have one's soul made by Charity into a shrine of God and a harbour of all truth is to achieve the Unitive Life, in which love becomes a permanent bond between the soul and God and is alone the soul's conscious guide in all things. To be qualified to give spiritual food to other souls is to be, like Piers, God's co-worker in the salvation of mankind, a prerogative only of those in a state of perfection. That the Highway's end is, indeed, the mystic's goal rather than that of the ordinary Christian is indicated by its being achieved only with the special permission of Grace. That Langland mentions grace only at this point, even though all the stages in the Highway obviously require it, indicates that the end is the work solely of grace, and grace in a special degree. Human effort can merit ordinary salvation, for which the required graces are not witheld; but human effort cannot merit contemplation, since only "uncreated Love," in Hilton's terms, can bring it about.[10] While mystical union has roots in human nature, its actual occurence depends solely on God's will as its cause.

The Highway also consists of the same principal means of humility and charity that Lady Church named:

---

[9] This is Elizabeth Zeeman's main point in her argument that the Highway leads to contemplation (*op. cit.*, pp. 3-7). She argues on the basis of parallels between Piers's Highway and Hilton's Pilgrimage. I shall argue on different grounds.

[10] *Scale*, II, 34, pp. 247-52.

Ac who so wol wende . ther as Treuthe dwelleth,
This ys the heye weye thyderwarde . wyteth wel the sothe.
ȝe most gon thorwe Mekenesse . all men and women,
Tyl ȝe come to Conscience . knowen of god selue,
That ys to seye sothliche . ȝe sholde rather deye
Than eny dedliche synne do . for drede other for preyere.
And thenne ȝoure neghebores next . in none wyse apeyre,
Other-wyse than ȝe wolde . thei wroughte ȝou all tymes.

(VIII:204-12)

This is the opening passage of the description of the Highway,
and it names the same virtues Lady Church named. In describing
the soul's love of God as one which stirs it to place God above all
things and die rather than commit deadly sin, Piers repeats the
words of Lady Church (II:143-44). And in admonishing the soul
to love his neighbor as well as God, Piers sums up Lady Church's
discussion of active charity (II:167-99). It should be noted that
this passage does not describe the first two steps of the Highway:
rather it names the two great legs of the entire way. Piers begins
with a general view of the road lying ahead before he describes
the particular steps. It should also be noted that Piers does not
detail at all the steps required to achieve Mekenesse. The Highway analyzes only the second leg, that of charity. The next line
after this passage, beginning "And so go forth by the brok"
(1. 213), initiates the description of the commandments, and
the commandments are simply a particularizing of the law of
charity. The first three commandments of the decalogue pertain
to the precept of love of God, the last seven pertain to the precept
of love of neighbor.[11] The relationship between Piers's Highway
and the rest of the poem is that it pertains to *Dobet* and *Dobest*,
which have to do with growth in charity culminating in a life of
union with God. It does not pertain to the *Visio* or *Dowel*, except to name the principal virtue of Mekenesse, the acquisition
of which governs these two parts of the poem. Although Piers's
instruction is more particular than Lady Church's, it still dwells

[11] I am paralleling the decalogue with the precept of charity according to
the decalogue's standard arrangement, not according to Langland's arrangement. Langland rearranges the usual order for a reason I cannot discern.
That the decalogue is a pre-statement of the law of charity is the standard
teaching of the Church, but see St. Thomas, *The Commandments of God*.

on the principle of love, and still looks well beyond what the soul has already achieved.

The particular steps of charity lead to salvation by the mystic's route. The best way to see this is to examine the stages both in light of the classic mystical way of purgation, illumination, and union, and in light of the beatitudes. The beatitudes are particularly applicable. Although the three stages of the mystic way were formulated as far back as St. Augustine, medieval mystics did not apply this terminology as rigidly as do moderns. It is unlikely that Langland had these three descriptive terms in mind when he organized either the Highway or the whole poem. They are convenient tools of analysis, however, and I shall employ them in this way. Langland may have been thinking of the beatitudes, on the other hand, since the steps of the Highway follow them fairly closely. In themselves the beatitudes, which lead the soul in a particular way to the beatific vision, are perfect works which only perfect souls can perform; but because they tell man where his true happiness lies, as opposed to what the maxims of the world tell him, they are instructive and inspiring to the Christian who seeks perfection but has not yet achieved it. Spiritual writers frequently organize, clarify, and give authority to their instructions by invoking the beatitudes, although not necessarily in their original order. In St. Bernard's *Of Conversion*, for example, which systematically discusses what a Christian must do even before he becomes a beginner, each step of the way is discussed in light of a corresponding beatitude. The imperfect soul cannot actually perform perfect works, but the works of the way to perfection may resemble the perfect works themselves.

The eight beatitudes listed in Matthew 5:3-12 are divided by St. Thomas into four groups: the first three, the next two, the two after these, and the last beatitude which is a confirmation and declaration of the preceding seven.[12] The first three are:

Blessed are the poor in spirit, for theirs is the kingdom of heaven.

---

[12] *Sum. Theo.*, I-II, q. 69, a. 3. My whole discussion of the beatitudes draws from this article and also from Garrigou-Lagrange, *op. cit.*, pp. 332-36.

Blessed are the meek, for they shall possess the earth. Blessed are they who mourn, for they shall be comforted.

(Verses 3-5)

These are the beatitudes of flight, so called because they pertain to deliverance from sin. Removing the falsity of the senses and their rebelliousness to reason, all three beatitudes are in a general way opposed to love of self. The first, blessed are the poor in spirit, concerns withdrawal from the affluence of external goods, both riches and honors, by learning to use them with moderation and, more excellently, by despising them altogether. The work of the *Visio* and *Dowel* corresponds to this beatitude, ending with complete withdrawal from external goods.[13] This is also the general message of the pardon in all three texts. Incidentally, the call to poverty does not necessarily mean that one must actually give up one's possessions, but that one must be poor in spirit. Langland does not insist that one take a vow of poverty or become a hermit; he is concerned about the inward condition of the soul. St. Thomas explains the relationship between poverty and perfection:

The renunciation of riches does not constitute perfection; it is merely a means to it. It is quite possible for a man to acquire perfection, without actually giving up what he possesses.[14]

Renunciation of one's possessions may be considered in two ways. First, as being actual: and thus it is not essential, but a means, to perfection . . . Hence nothing hinders the state of perfection from being without renunciation of one's possessions, and the same applies to other outward practices. Secondly, it may be considered in relation to one's preparedness, in the sense of being prepared to renounce or give away all: and this belongs directly to perfection.[15]

The second beatitude, blessed are the meek, also concerns flight from sin and purification of the sensual part of man's nature. Strictly taken, meekness is the virtue which overcomes the irascible passions by keeping them within the bounds of reason so

[13] Piers calls for a resolution not to be so busy about the world in the B-text (VIII:117-29), but actual abandonment is not achieved by other souls until passus 17 of the C-text, just before the appearance of *Liberum Arbitrium*.

[14] *The Religious State*, 18, p. 99.

[15] *Sum. Theo.*, II-II, q. 184, a. 7, rep. obj. 1.

that one is undisturbed by them. It results in calmness, serenity, entire submission to God's will. In the broad sense, meekness includes humility, not only because both meekness and humility are parts of temperance, but also because they are associated in Christ's appeal to men, an appeal of first importance to those seeking to be "like oure Lorde": "Take my yoke upon you, and learn from me, for I am meek and humble of heart; and you will find rest for your souls" (Matt. 12:29). Thus St. Bernard writes:

I am, saith He, The Way and the Truth and the Life. He calls humility 'the way' because it leads to the truth. In the former lies the labour, in the latter is the reward. But, you may ask, how am I to know that He was here speaking of humility, since He says without further explanation, I am the Way? Listen to His more explicit statement, Learn of me because I am meek and humble of heart. In this He exhibits Himself as a type of humility, a model of meekness.[16]

Again, both the Visio and Dowel are governed by the requirements of Meekness, especially Dowel, which concerns flight from sin through eradicating weaknesses of the spirit. One of the major personifications in Dowel, and the last to be present before the appearance of Liberum Arbitrium, is Patience, whose definition is significant:

'What is parfit Pacience?' . quath Activa uita.
'Meeknesse and mylde speche . and men of one wil,
The whiche wil loue ledeth . to oure lordes place;
And that is Charite, chaumpion . chief of alle vertues,
And that is poure pacient . alle perilis to suffre."

(XVI:276-80)

The third beatitude of flight, blessed are they who mourn, concerns sorrow in two ways, the second more perfect than the first. One is to shed the tears of holy contrition, having seen the gravity of sin as a spiritual evil and an offense against God. The other is to make a deliberate choice of sorrow by withdrawing from concupiscible passions through restricting them to moderate satisfactions or through renouncing them altogether. The work corresponding to the first sense of this beatitude is dramatized directly

---

[16] The Twelve Degrees of Humility and Pride, trans. by R. V. Mills London, 1929), p. 9.

in the Confessions of the Seven Deadly Sins (VI:109-VIII:154), and that corresponding to the second and more excellent sense is Patience's conversation with *Active uita* (XVI:185-XVII:157), which culminates with a sermon on how poverty helps defend against the seven sins.[17]

Since the details of the Highway do not concern what takes place in the *Visio* and *Dowel*, Piers does not give steps which correspond to the first three beatitudes. Instead, he merely says that Meknesse is one of the two general stages the soul must go through. In name, however, this virtue alludes to the second of the three beatitudes of flight, and in meaning it includes all of them. As can be seen from the already quoted opening passage of the Highway (VIII:204-12), this virtue has a broad meaning. Meknesse, Piers says, leads to a clear conscience: one that loves nothing more than or equally with God; one whose love of God keeps it free from sin even in the face of threats or appeals from other persons; and one which fulfills the precept of charity by loving God and neighbor above all else. Such a conscience presupposes that the sensual part of man has been moderated to the point of being no hindrance to love of God and neighbor, that the will cannot be turned from its true object even in difficult situations, and that pride, the source of all sin, has been extinguished. That meekness includes humility is clear from the phrase, "Conscience knowen of god selue", which alludes to those passages, also in the Sermon on the Mount,[18] where Christ admonishes men not to make shows of fasting or almsgiving in order to impress men, but to maintain a secret purity, "a penaunce discret", to quote from Will's explanation of what Christ really wants (VI:84). The meekness Piers describes includes the works corresponding to all of the first three beatitudes, and all that is generally understood to be involved in first conversion and the purgative way, or the way of the beginner.

The remainder of the road, analyzing the way of charity,

---

[17] In the B-version *Activa uita* washes the sins out of his cloak, but in the C-version the description of the sins is transfered to the Confessions in the *Visio*.

[18] Matt. 6, *passim*.

follows the beatitudes in order. One must go through the commandments and cross the moat of mercy (VII:211-233), each
of which corresponds to the next two beatitudes:

Blessed are they who hunger and thirst for justice, for they shall be
satisfied. Blessed are the merciful, for they shall obtain mercy.
(Verses 6-7)

All the precepts of the decalogue pertain to justice.[19] If Piers urges
the folk to press on through the commandments, it is not because
they are of the Old Law.[20] They are of the New Law as well. It is
rather because in the way of perfection fulfilling the precepts is
not enough, and also because the beatitude speaks of hungering
and thirsting after their fulfillment. But the thirst for justice must
not become a bitter zeal with regard either to oneself or to the
guilty; hence, the work of the next beatitude is to ask for merciful
forgiveness of one's own sins, and to show mercy by being attentive to the sufferings of others. The union of justice and mercy
is difficult because they seem opposed. Achieving harmony between them is already evidence of the presence of God in the
soul, for He alone can unite them intimately. These two virtues,
furthermore, like the beatitudes to which they correspond, are of
the active life insofar as they involve one's relations to his neighbors. By justice one does his duty to his neighbors, by mercy one
grants spontaneous favors in his neighbor's behalf. The Samaritan,
representing the theological virtue of charity in the *Vita* (XX:
46-93), vividly dramatizes the acts of these virtues, and the Four
Daughters dramatize the harmonizing of these virtues in Will
(XXI:115-272, 458-71).

Having crossed the moat of mercy, one must then ride to
A-mend-ʒow with a contrite heart and a willingness to do penance.
Then one must humble himself before Grace and beseech him to
open the gates that Adam and Eve have shut. If Grace permits
entrance, then one shall see God in his own heart (VIII:248-55).
These steps, amends and winning the grace that opens heaven's
gates, correspond to the next two beatitudes:

[19] *Sum. Theo.,* II-II, q. 122, a. 1.
[20] As Father Dunning seems to suggest: *Interpretation of the A-text,*
p. 122.

Blessed are the clean of heart, for they shall see God. Blessed are the peacemakers, for they shall be called children of God.

(Verses 8-9)

A clean heart is necessary for a vision of God because it is sin that obscures the divine image in man. When sin is cleansed away and the soul has made its peace with God, it lives in harmony with both God and man; it has a conscience that offends neither God nor men. It also communicates this peace to others. Guided solely by charity, the soul loses all egoism and makes a veritable church of itself in that it keeps itself pure so that God may dwell in it, and by work and example it brings other souls into God's presence. The two works of these beatitudes still pertain to the active life, but the rewards, that one sees God and is a child of God, pertain to the contemplative life. Will achieves this goal in passus 22, when, going to communion and confession, he has a vision of the suffering Christ and of the Paraclete who descends to found the Church.

The steps from the commandments to the sight of God belong roughly to the illuminative stage, or the stage of the proficient, with contemplation the entrance into the unitive stage. In the illuminative stage one advances in virtue, both moral – which concerns relations with other men – and theological – which concerns relations with God. Having subdued its sensual part in the purgative stage, the soul now purifies its intellectual part through coming to understand the misery of other men. It does this by considering the suffering of men in general, but most of all by considering the humanity of Christ, who is the model of suffering, righteousness, mercy, and a compassion that leads one to lay down his life for his neighbor. Love is strengthened, prayers are affective in being charged with love, and the soul is cleansed so that one is disposed to contemplation.

Piers's description of the court includes, in one way or another, matters pertaining particularly to the illuminative stage, but also to the unitive. The works of each stage never disappear, but culminate in the Unitive Life, where all works of penance and virtue are done harmoniously. But the last two stages contrast with the first in being positive rather than negative; the promotion of good predominates over the extermination of evil. One begins to be an active Christian in the illuminative stage, where the motivation is hope of salvation rather than fear of damnation.

> Al the wallynge ys of Wit . for Wil ne sholde hit wynne.
> The kernels beth of Crystendome . that kynde to saue,
> And boteraced with By-leyue-so- . other-thow-best-nat-
> saued.
> Alle the houses beth heled . halles and chambres,
> With no lede, bote with Loue . and with Leel-speche.
> The barres aren of Buxumnesse . as brethren of one wombe.
> The brigge hatte Bid-wel- . the-bet-myght-thow-spede;
> Eche pyler ys of Penaunce . and preyers to seyntes,
> The hokes aren Almys-dedes . that the ʒates hongen on.
>
> (VIII:234-42)

The term *Wil* cannot refer to the intellective appetite, since this is the motivating faculty in man and the subject of charity, thus never ceasing to be the focal point of inward development. *Wil* refers to the carnal appetites, which must be subjected to the intellective power, namely, Wit, before God's kingdom is established in the soul. The battlements of Christendom "that kynde to saue" refer to the illuminative stage as the point at which one becomes an active follower of Christ as well as a frequent meditator on Christ's humanity. In this sense one begins truly to be a Christian and sees Christendom as offering hope of salvation. The term *illuminative* suggests that in this stage one has left the darkness of sin and begins to see the light of salvation.[21]

The walls are buttressed by Faith, the roofs covered by Love and Loyal Speech, and the bolts are of "Buxumnesse . as brethren of one wombe". All of these emphasize the habit of virtue, which is the aim of this stage, especially of the infused theological virtues by which a soul may act in a superhuman rather than a human manner.[22] The heroic practice of virtue is possible in the illuminative stage, although not usually achieved until the unitive. The virtue of Hope is implied by such statements as "that kynde to saue", and "By-leyue-so-other-thow-best-nat-saued", which in-

---

[21] See Pascal Parente, *The Ascetical Life*, p. 113.
[22] *Sum. Theo.*, I-II, q. 62, a. 1.

dicate that salvation is in sight, and hope of it is the chief motivation. "By-leyue-so . . ." adds Faith, Love adds Charity. Langland must have in mind the habit of these virtues, their constant infusion, rather than their ordinary possession, for without the latter mode of possession one could not achieve even the state of meekness that Piers describes. Leel-speche and Buxumnesse are the principal acts of Love, the first referring to the first precept of charity, the second to the second precept. Since Loyal Speech has the importance of being coordinate with Love, in that both are the roofs of all the halls and chambers, I take Loyal Speech to mean prayers of praise and allegiance to God, or the affective prayer characteristic of this stage. The effect of love is to burst forth into praise of God and confessions of loyalty, which in turn is a manifestation of adherence to the first precept of charity.[23] "Buxumnesse . as brethren of one wombe," or fraternal love, has less status than "Leel-speche" because the second precept of charity derives from the first precept:

Thus, the perfection of the spiritual life consists, primarily and principally, in the love of God . . . The perfection of the spiritual life consists, secondarily, in the love of our neighbor.[24]

Still, fraternal love is not an option, but an obligation for perfect and imperfect alike. Not only is the precept of charity not fulfilled unless one loves his neighbor, but fraternal love is firm proof of one's love of God. Hence, "Buxumnesse" is described as the bolts which hold the roof in place.

This much of Piers's description concerns the court proper. The remainder concerns the bridge over the moat of Mercy and the entranceway, and thus returns to the means of advancing. The bridge is "Bid-wel-the-bet-myght-thow-spede", the pillars are of "Penaunce . and preyers to seyntes," and the hinges of the gate are of "Almys-dedes". All of these have already been explained as involving work parallel to the sixth beatitude: blessed are the clean of heart. Together with prayers to the saints, "Bidwel" refers to prayers of petition or vocal prayer, which the per-

[23] See Richard of St. Victor, *Benjamin Minor*, XII (*P. L.*, 196, coll. 8C-9D).
[24] St. Thomas, *The Religious State*, II, pp. 8-9.

fect by no means cease to practice, and has specifically to do with expressions of contrition and requests for merciful forgiveness. Bid-wel alludes to "Ask, and it shall be given you; seek, and you shall find; knock, and it shall be opened to you", a passage from the Sermon on the Mount again in which Christ speaks of prayers (Matt. 7:7). Almsdeeds, finally, are a traditional form of penance and are specific works of mercy.

The end of the Highway is the Unitive Life, in which the soul is God's tabernacle and a peacemaker among men and between God and man. Even though one has now tasted the heavenly fruit, this is the most difficult life because all the preceding work must still be maintained while one labors amidst the hazards of the world, and because one is susceptible to pride in his own perfection:

> Be war thenne of Wratthe . that wickede shrewe,
> For he hath enuye to hym . that in thyn herte sytteth,
> And poketh forth pruyde . to preysy thi-selue.
> The boldness of thy bynfet . maketh the blynde thenne,
> So worst thow dryuen out as deuh . and the dore closed,
> Y-keyed and yclyketed . to close the with-oute,
> Haplich and hondred wynter . are thow eft entrie.
> Thus myght thou lese hus loue . to lete wel by thi-selue,
> And geten hit a-geyn thorw grace . ac thorgh no gifte elles.
>
> (VIII:261-69)

In warning specifically against Wratthe as the principal enemy of the soul in the unitive way, Piers may have several scriptural passages in mind:

> He who says that he is in the light, and hates his brother, is in the darkness still. He who loves his brother abides in the light, and for him there is no stumbling. But he who hates his brother is in the darkness, and walks in the darkness, and he does not know whither he goes; because the darkness has blinded his eyes.
>
> (I John 2:9-11)

> But I say to you that everyone who is angry with his brother shall be liable to judgment; and whoever says to his brother, "Raca,' shall be liable to the Sanhedrin; and whoever says, 'Thou fool!,' shall be liable to the fire of Gehennna.
>
> (Matt. 5:22)

The second passage is from the Sermon on the Mount, and it reminds us of the reason why wrath, of all possible vices, is the one which may bring the almost perfected soul down. Just as the Unitive Life sustains all the work of perfection but in difficult circumstances, so the last beatitude sums up all the preceding and emphasizes the kinds of difficulties one faces in fulfilling them:

Blessed are they who suffer persecution for justice' sake, for theirs is the kingdom of heaven. Blessed are you when men reproach you, and persecute you, and, speaking falsely, say all manner of evil against you, for my sake. Rejoice and exult, because your reward is great in heaven; for so did they persecute the prophets who were before you.

(Verses 10-12)

To respond in anger to one's persecutors, and concomitantly to indulge in a sense of pride in one's own perfection, is to lose all. Anger and pride destroy meekness and humility, the first stage of the highway and the foundation of perfection. As meekness leads one to charity, so anger and pride destroy charity, particularly because, having tasted the heavenly fruit, the perfect soul has the strongest reasons for, and the strongest possibility of, not succumbing to these circumstances. Piers therefore warns that such a fallen soul will never be restored to God's love unless God Himself restores the soul by a special act. If one should fall, Piers says, it may be a hundred years before one re-enters, and then only through grace, "ac thorgh no gifte eles". The author of the Epistle to the Hebrews is equally emphatic:

For it is impossible for those who were once enlightened, who have both tasted the heavenly gift and become partakers of the Holy Spirit, who have moreover tasted the good word of God and the powers of the world to come, and then have fallen away, to be renewed again to repentance; since they crucify again for themselves the Son of God and make him a mockery. For the earth that drinks in the rain that often falls upon it, and produces vegetation that is of use to those by whom it is tilled, receives a blessing from God; but that which brings forth thorns and thistles is worthless, and is nigh unto a curse, and its end is to be burnt.

(Heb. VI:4-8)

In the last passus of *Dobest*, and of the poem, Langland develops at length the many kinds of persecution, particularly pride, the soul must resist, its necessity to resist without damaging its sanctity, and its need, in the midst of persecution, always to pursue charity.

After he outlines the way to perfection, Piers speaks of the Seven Sisters who guard the posterns. He is not speaking now of the soul who has fallen from perfection, for such a one, he has said, can do nothing to restore himself to God's love. Piers is speaking to the people who have not yet truly been converted:

> 'Ho is not sib to these seuene . sothly to telle,
> Hit is ful hard, by myn heued . eny of ȝou alle
> To geten ingang at eny gate . bote grace be the more.'
>
> (VIII:280-82)

Piers is reminding the people, in effect, that not only must they confirm their rejection of the Seven Deadly Sins before they can enter into the way of perfection, they must also be kin to the seven corresponding virtues. Many of the people refuse, re-enacting the parable of the feast; but Contemplacion does not refuse (VIII:283-308). Here Langland alludes to the active and contemplative lives in order to make the point that he who is unprepared to give over the affairs of the world will be frightened from perfection by the difficulty of the way; but whoever has the spirit of a contemplative will not be deterred by the austerity that lies ahead. The significance for us of the appearance of Actif and Contemplacion at this point is that we have one more proof, to be added to what I have already said, that the Highway, and *Piers Plowman*, concerns perfection rather than simple salvation.

VIII. CONCLUSIONS

Both Lady Church's sermon and Piers's description of the Highway to Truth, wherein the question of salvation is directly and
fundamentally answered, are substantially identical in thought
and wording to corresponding passages in all three texts. The
conclusion seems inescapable, therefore, assuming my analysis
to be valid, that all three versions are concerned with the mystic's
way of salvation rather than that of the ordinary Christian, and
that each version must be interpreted in this light. And since the
question of perfection arises at the very beginning of the poem
rather than only in its later stages, existing interpretations of
whatever text, insofar as they are valid, must be considered as
explicating subsidiary themes of *Piers Plowman* rather than its
central theme. Indeed, if my argument be subject only to refine-
ment and not complete destruction, a fresh interpretation, I feel,
is needed, and a synoptic interpretation is possible. The key to a
detailed understanding of Langland's poem lies in those medieval
works that develop the psychology of the mystic's way. All the
spiritual tracts and sermons of St. Bernard should prove of primary value, but especially his *Of Conversion*, which throws considerable light on the *Visio*, including the Pardon scene, and his
Steps of Humility and Pride, which sheds equally abundant
light on the *Vita*. This latter treatise explains the basic general
steps of humility and charity as involved in the way of perfection and mystical union, and the steps themselves of humility
and pride generally parallel Will's progress in *Dowel*, beginning
with his dream-within-a-dream in passus 12 and ending with
Liberum Arbitrium's sermon on curiosity in passus 17. Richard

of St. Victor's *Benjamin Minor* is another very popular work of the Middle Ages which should prove valuable for interpreting the poem from the Confessions in passus 6 to the end of *Dobet*.

The conclusion that all three versions were written by a single author also gains support from the thesis of this study. To Donaldson's thorough argument in favor of single authorship must be added the observations that the allegorical method of all three versions is consistent, Will's character and aspirations are unchanged, and the spiritual basis of each version is identical. Without going beyond the purpose of establishing the context in which *Piers Plowman* ought to be read, this study has suggested interpretations of certain parts of the poem in order to show that perfection is not only its expressed subject, but also the subject it develops. If *Piers* is the result of multiple authorship, then subsequent authors were remarkable in their ability to continue the individual style, the personality, and the method of the original, and in their having understood the original author very well. A detailed interpretation made in light of the medieval mystical tradition, I am confident, will prove it even more unlikely that several individuals could have achieved such complete unanimity of mind and spirit.

If the thesis of this study has been validly argued, finally, the view that the A-text comprises two separate and complete poems must be rejected. The only evidence for the independence of the A-*Vita* from the A-*Visio* is that offered by both Father Dunning and David Fowler: that in all A-MSS the *Visio* ends with the colophon: "Explicit hic visio Willelmi de Petro Plouʒman, et incipit Vita de Dowel, Dobet, et Dobest secundum wyt et resoun", and that the numbering of the *Vita* begins over from the beginning.[1] This is precious little and not very striking. The colophon and numbering are justified because the *Visio* and *Vita* are the two great parts of a single poem. *The Divine Comedy*, for example, is a single work, and each of its three parts has its own name and numbering. Yet one would not consider the *Inferno, Purgatorio,* and *Paradiso* three independent poems. The B and

---

[1] Dunning, *Interpretation of the A-Text,* pp. 4-5, 167-69; Fowler, *op. cit.,* pp. 4-7.

C-versions, which Father Dunning believes were written by the same author, have colophons and headings which emphasize the connection between the *Visio* and *Vita* rather than their separation. In the C-version, and partly in the B, *Dowel, Dobet,* and *Dobest* have both separate titles and separate numbering, yet each of these parts does not seem a separate poem. Besides, Dunning observes that the two parts are connected at the end of the *Visio* by the problem of Dowel, and Fowler goes even further, claiming that the question of the value of learning, urged as the subject of A-*Vita,* is raised in the dispute between Piers and the Priest.[2] These observations tend to contradict their already thin argument for independence, for in view of these connections the urgency of the problem of learning and the motivation for pursuing it are lost of the *Vita* is read without first reading the end of the *Visio*. Unless one somehow assume Langland had it in mind all along to write two independent but inseparable poems, this contradiction is not resolved by calling the A-*Vita* a sequel.[3]

The evidence offered for considering A[2] complete and self-sufficient is even less convincing than that offered for separation. Both Dunning and Fowler argue at some length for the exclusion of the "John But passus" from the A-*Vita*,[4] but granting them that, the only reason they have for assuming the completeness of the rest of A[2] is that without the "John But Passus" it ends on a note of finality. But many passus in *Piers Plowman* end on a note of finality. If, for example, we had only the first two passus of this poem, assuming the remainder of it to have been lost, we might reasonably conclude on the basis of the finality-test that these two passus comprised a complete work. If we had only the first five passus, taking us through the Meed episode, we might again see no need for further discussion. In short, it is part of Langland's general manner to close off one section climactically and begin another abruptly. Thus there is

---

[2] *Ibid.,* Dunning, p. 167; Fowler, pp. 9-16.
[3] As Dunning does, *ibid.,* p. 167.
[4] *Ibid.,* Dunning, pp. 167-69; Fowler, pp. 4-7. Fowler also argues this point in his *Piers Plowman: A Critical Edition of the A-Version* (Baltimore, 1952), pp. 148-50, 170 (n. 117), 252.

no basis for assuming that A² was meant to have nothing beyond it. And since the interpretations offered by Dunning and Fowler absolutely depend on the assumption of two separate and complete poems in the A-text, their interpretations are not acceptable insofar as they purport to develop the "true" subjects of the A-text. The problems of *temporalia* and learning are unquestionably raised in this poem, and not only in the parts to which Dunning and Fowler confine them; but they are subsidiary themes involved in the larger subject of salvation through perfection.

The foregoing study, on the other hand, has given positive reasons for taking the *Visio* and *Vita* as two successive parts of the same work in all three texts, and for considering the A-version, no matter where it ends, as incomplete. The scheme of salvation expressed in all three versions is not fulfilled until perfection is reached. The spiritual foundation laid by Lady Church and Piers in the three texts is too large to support only the *Visio,* or, for that matter, any segment of the poem this side of *Dobest.* The character of the Dreamer, furthermore, who wishes actually to be saved rather than be told about his salvation, requires that the poem take him to the point where he knows Truth "kyndely". If the *Vita* did not continue the work of the *Visio,* and if Dobest were not the natural and necessary culmination of Will's search, then Langland could be accused of having created a character only to frustate him, and of having taught the way to scale a mountain, but led the way merely over the foothills.

As has already been suggested, the experience Will seeks is achieved in the Vision of Christ. In the *Visio* and *Dowel,* he undergoes what is necessary to achieve humility in the broad sense of including all that is contrary to self-love. The *Visio* concerns eradication of the relatively superficial bodily causes of self-love, and is roughly equivalent to first conversion; *Dowel* concerns eradication of the deepest propensities, both bodily and spiritual, toward self-love, and is the equivalent of purgation or what is sometimes called 'true' conversion. The *Visio* is simply a preparation for *Dowel,* wherein humility is sought consciously. With the appearance of *Liberum Arbitrium* in the last passus of *Dowel* (XVII:158 ff.), Will undergoes the transition from the "school of humility" to the "school of charity".[5] All of *Dobet* then concerns growth in charity, culminating with the vision of the Passion and the Harrowing of Hell (Passus 21). In this vision, a form of preliminary contemplation which might better be called meditation,[6] Will achieves the

> ... kynde knowyng . that kenneth in thyn herte
> For to louye thy lord . leuest of alle,
> And deye rathere than to do . eny dedlich synne.
>
> (II:141-44)

Here Will receives justification and peace, is henceforth able to rule himself both "sweetly" and mightily", and his soul is prepared to receive the gift of contemplation. In the first passus of *Dobest* (Passus 22), Will achieves the conscious awareness of the life of Grace which constitutes contemplation proper.[7] In this vision he sees briefly Christ bearing the cross, contemplates the divine name of Christ as opposed to the human name of Jesus, and sees the Paraclete descend to distribute gifts among men and establish the Church. As is consistent with Langland's method of depicting a public event in order both to criticize his times and dramatize allegorically what takes place inwardly in the individual soul, the

---

[5] Thus the B-version begins a new passus at this point, passus 15, which Skeat calls "Prologue to Do-bet" and which has the heading: "Passus xv^us: finit Dowel, et incipit Dobet".

[6] Meditation on the Passion of Christ, and devotion to the humanity of Christ in general, are traditionally regarded as the proximate preparation for contemplation. See Gilson, *The Mystical Theology of St. Bernard*, pp. 80-84, where this point is discussed with ample references to Bernard's works. See also Hilton's *Scale*, I, chaps. 15, 35, 36.

[7] I wish to emphasize that I use the term *contemplation* in the sense already defined and as the goal which Lady Church has indicated. Scientifically, many distinctions can be made between degrees of contemplation, and there is still controversy concerning the nature of the contemplative experience. I leave the scientific analysis of the experience depicted in Langland to theologians. Just as some theologians nowadays believe that Richard Rolle never achieved "pure" contemplation, even though he himself believed he did, so it may turn out, in the view of some, that Langland does not dramatize the "highest" and "purest" form of contemplation achievable by man. But some form of contemplation, I feel certain, and one which fulfills the teaching of this poem, takes place here.

descent of the Paraclete fulfills Lady Church's promise that

> . . . to knowe it kyndeliche . hit comseth by myghte,
> In the herte, ther is the hefd . and the hye welle.
> Of kynde knowyng in herte . ther comseth a myghte,
> That falleth to the fader . that formede ous alle.
>
> (II:160-63)

Passus 23, the last of the poem, then dramatizes the difficulties one faces in the Unitive Life and the need constantly to pursue charity and perfection while one lives in this world.

Our understanding of Langland's depiction of the Vision of Christ has perenially been complicated by three things: (1) the loose but unmistakable historical chronology this part of the poem follows in moving from the Crucifixion to Pentecost: (2) the drama of the Four Daughters and Book which surrounds the Harrowing of Hell (XXI:115-272, 458-71); (3) and the appearance of Piers as confusingly like Christ (XXII:1-14). But these three elements are not only explained by Langland's spirituality as I have developed it, they are also the prime evidence that, allegorically, this section of the poem dramatizes Will's coming to perfection, contemplation, and a life of union with God.

Besides having its own historical logic, the Vision of Christ follows the psychological process which occurs at this stage of the soul's spiritual growth. The immediate preparation for contemplation is the remembrance or meditation on the Passion and Resurrection of Christ, for these reveal forcefully God's love for the soul, thereby evoking an outpouring of the soul's love for God. Enlarged in charity, the soul is prepared to receive the indwelling of the Word. "For where He perceives that the grace of His passion or the glory of His Resurrection is pondered as the subject of diligent meditation, there straightway He is present with eagerness and joy." [8] Thus Will awakens from this vision in a state of heightened devotion. His love of God is now completely aware of itself, his confidence in Christ's continuing presence and aid is unshakeable, and his praise of God is open and direct:

[8]   St. Bernard, *On the Necessity of Loving God*, iii, p. 237.

Tyl the day dawede . these damseles daunsede,
Than men rang to the resurreccioun . and with that
   ich awakede,
And kallyde Kytte my wyf . and Kalote my doughter,
'A rys, and go reuerence . godes resurreccioun,
And creop on kneos to the croys . and cusse hit for a Iuwel,
And rightfullokest a relyk . non richer on erthe.
For godes blesside body . hit bar for oure bote,
And hit a-fereth the feonde . for such is the myghte,
May no grysliche gost . glyde ther hit shadeweth!'

                                  (XXI:471-79)

Immediately afterward, at the opening of *Dobest*, Will awakens,

And dyhte me derly . and dude me to churche,
To huyre holliche the masse . and be housled after.
In myddes of the masse . tho men ȝeden to offrynge,
Ich fel eft-sones a-slepe . . .

                                  (XXII:2-5)

and has a contemplative vision. His brief description of himself, taken in the context of how he felt after meditating on the Passion and Resurrection, expresses curtly what St. Bernard expresses fully in his description of the circumstances under which the soul receives the gift of contemplation:

. . . if you shall enter into the House of prayer in solitude and collectedness of spirit, if your mind be thoughtful and free of worldly cares, and if standing in the Presence of God before some altar, you shall touch, as it were, the portal of heaven with the hand of holy aspiration and longing; if, having been brought among the choirs of the saints by the fervour of your devotion (for the prayer of the righteous soul can scale even the heights of heaven), you deplore before them, in deep humility, your spiritual troubles and miseries, you plead your necessities with frequent sighs and groans too deep for utterance, and entreat earnestly their compassion; if, I say, you act thus, I have full confidence in Him who said: *Ask, and ye shall receive* (Matt. vii, 7), and I believe that if you persevere in knocking earnestly at the door, it shall certainly be opened to you, and you shall not go away empty.[9]

The cruxifixion, furthermore, is the model and inspiration for mortification of the flesh, necessary for contemplation because the fleshly desires stand as a barrier between the soul and

---

[9] Sermon XLIX, 3, on the *Canticle*.

Christ, and for the willing acceptance of adversity. "And they who belong to Christ have crucified their flesh with its passions and desires" (Gal. 5:24). Mortification helps turn love of self into love of God, with the result, in Bernardian spirituality, that freedom from sin and from misery are regained as far as possible on earth, and the divine likeness in man is restored. Meditating on the Life of Christ, the individual is inspired with a new motive for bearing the afflictions of mortification and adversity: the desire to participate in Christ's suffering on the cross, his ransoming of sinners, and his redemption of mankind. "His sufferings have become, in the fullest sense of the term, a *compassion* with the Passion of Christ." [10] Meditation results in the individual's willing and joyful acceptance of painful afflictions; he willingly takes up his cross. Thus the first thing Will sees in his contemplative vision is Christ, resembling Piers, painted all bloody, "And cam yn with a croys" (XXII:6-7). Will is able to see this because he, himself, has achieved this state: "God will then appear towards you, such as you shall have appeared towards Him." [11] In fact, Will's achieving contemplation during the Eucharistic offering suggests both the willing participation in Christ's suffering, which prepares the soul for the mystical experience, and the reception of God in the soul, which constitutes it:

But why should we not understand the expressions, "eat My Flesh" and "drink My Blood", as an injunction to participate in His sufferings and imitate the example which He has given us in the flesh? The same lesson is taught us in the most holy Sacrament of the altar, wherein we receive the Lord's Body; that, as in this mystery, the species of bread visibly enters our bodies, so we may know that, by the example of His earthly life, the Lord Himself comes into us invisibly to "dwell by faith in our hearts". For when justice enters our souls, He also enters "Who of God is made unto us justice', as St. Paul speaks. And according to St. John, "He that abideth in charity, abideth in God and God in Him.[12]

Will manifests this characteristic strikingly in the very last pas-

[10] Gilson, *The Mystical Theology of St. Bernard*, p. 84.
[11] St. Bernard, Sermon LXIX, 7, on the *Canticle*.
[12] St. Bernard, Third Sermon on Ps. XC, in *Sermons*, I, pp. 150-51.

sus of the poem. Having returned to the world and its cares, Will is ailing in heart, "For ich ne wist wher to ete . ne in what place" (XXIII:3). At noon he meets Neode (XXIII:4-50), who argues validly that necessity has no law, but Will does not exercise his prerogative of getting food any way he can. Later, asleep, he is attacked by Elde, who gallops straight over his head. Will feels the pains of old age, for "ich sat in this sorwe" (XXIII:199), but the cheerfulness and downright humor of his complaint are unmistakable, manifesting in the midst of affliction a light-heartedness not exhibited in him before:

'Syre vuel-ytauht Elde,' quath ich . 'vnhende go with
    the!'
Suthte whanne was the hey wey . ouer menne hefdes?
Haddest thow be hende,' quath ich . 'thow woldest haue
    asked leue!'
'3e! leue lordeyn!' quath he . and leyde on me with age,
And hitte me vnder the ere . vnnethe may ich huyre.
He boffatede me a-boute the mouthe . and bete oute my
    wangteth,
And gyuede me with goutes . ich may not go at large.
And of the wo that ich was yn . my wif hadde reuthe,
And wisshede wel witerlyche . that ich were in heuene.
For the lyme that she louede me for . and leef was to
    feele,
And a nyghtes namelich . when we naked were,
Ich ne myghte in none manere . maken hit at heore
    wille,
So Elde and hue hit hadde . a-feynted and forbete.
                                         (XXIII:186-98)

The reward for meditative devotion to the humanity of Christ is a mystical experience in which the Holy Spirit bestows on the soul gratuitous gifts. Necessary gifts of the Holy Spirit are those which sanctify the soul in order that it may be saved. Gratuitous gifts are given for the profit and good of others.[13] These qualify the soul as God's co-worker; indeed, they obligate the soul to return from contemplation to the labours of the active life among men. The reception of these gifts is likened to the Pente-

13   The scriptural basis for this doctrine is I Cor. 12. See also St. Bernard, Sermon XVIII, 1, on the *Canticle*.

cost. In fact, since the soul is enlightened in some particular way by the Holy Spirit, and since the purpose of the gift is to enable the soul to contribute to the needs of the Mystical Body, it is a re-enactment of the Pentecost.[14] The reception of these gifts by the soul, finally, is an indispensable sign, according to St. Bernard, that some form of contemplation has been reached. If these gifts are accompanied by spiritual understanding and fervent zeal, then the soul may justifiably feel it has reached the highest form of contemplation.[15] In *Piers Plowman*, this experience is dramatized in the first passus of Dobest (XXII:199-382).

> On *spiritus paraclitus* . to Peers and to hus felawes,
> In liknesse of a lyghtnynge . a-lyghte on hem alle,
> And made hem conne and knowe . alle kynne languages.
> Ich wondrede what that was . and waggede Conscience,
> And was a-fered for the lyght . for in fuyres lyknesse
> *Spiritus paraclitus* . ouer-spradde hem alle.
>
> (XXII:201-206)

The gifts that the Paraclete dispenses are all gratuitous gifts and meant to supply the needs of the Mystical Body. The establishing of the Church dramatizes objectively what is subjectively happening to Will, and what Piers described as the goal of the Highway to Truth:

> Al-so charge Charyte . a churche to make
> In thyn hole herte . to herberghwen alle treuthe,
> And fynde alle manere folke . fode to hure saules,
> Yf loue and leaute . and owre lawe by trewe.
>
> (VIII:257-60)

The drama of the Four Daughters also indicates that Will's vision of Christ dramatizes his reaching a spiritual state of perfection, and is prepared for the gift of contemplation. The Four Daughters allegorize the change taking place in Will's spiritual condition as the result of meditation on the Passion. Lady Church has said at the beginning of the poem that when the heart sees that love is the "tryacle for synne", the "soueryne salue" for soul and body, and the "plonte of pees", it naturally

---

[14] See St. Bernard, Sermon XLIX, 1-2, on the *Canticle*.
[15] *Ibid.*, paragraphs 3-4.

embraces love with its fruits of justification and peace, both of which refer to the establishing of interior harmony in the purified soul. The disputation among the Daughters (XXI:115-272) and their reconciliation in the end (XXI:458-71) dramatize allegorically Will's achievement of true sanctity, which Garrigou-Langrange defines as "perfect purity, immutable union with God, and also the intimate harmony of all the virtues, even of those which to all appearances are most opposed",[16] and his preparation to receive Christ in his heart. In his Eleventh Sermon on Ps. XC, St. Bernard discusses the ways of the Lord, and specifically the way in which Christ comes to souls:

"All the ways of the Lord are mercy and truth." It is by these ways, my brethren, that He comes to all souls in general and to each in particular, viz., by the ways of mercy and truth. For we cannot suppose that God has yet come to him, who, whilst presuming much on His mercy, seems to have forgotten His justice or truth. But neither is He found in the heart which is filled with terror by the remembrance of His truth, without deriving any consolation from the thought of His mercy. *He* cannot be said to hold the truth, who fails to recognise mercy where it truly exists: on the other hand mercy, to be true, must be accompanied by truth, that is to say, by justice. Accordingly, where (as the Psalmist sings) "Mercy and truth have met each other, (there) justice and peace have kissed." Nor can the Lord Himself be far away since "His place is in peace."[17]

Here is the precedent for Langland's use of verse 10 from Psalm 85. Contemplating the truth and justice of Christ, as well as his mercy in redeeming souls from Hell, Will achieves a spiritual awareness and love that effects an interior reconciliation of these virtues in him, and thus readies his soul for Christ.

This interpretation of the Four Daughters passages is supported by the appearance of Book (XXI:240-70). Book's allegorical purpose is to verify the meditative vision as coming from God rather than from the Devil or some other false cause. The validity of visions was a common problem among medieval mystics, and the means of verifying them were widely discussed. The test Langland calls upon is one of the most basic: Scripture

---

[16] *Op. cit.*, p. 178.
[17] In *Sermons*, I, pp. 239-40.

itself. It is the test urged by Richard of St. Victor in a chapter of his *Benjamin Minor*, which discusses visions coming before contemplation proper, and which bears the caption: *"Quam suspecta debeat esse omnis revelatio, quam non comitatur Scripturarum attestatio."*[18] Literally, Book settles the argument among the Daughters by recounting the supernatural and miraculous ocurrences that accompanied Christ's life and death and that testify to Christ's divinity and therefore his authority in the Harrowing of Hell. Allegorically, he is the device by which Langland goes through the formality of indicating that Will is experiencing a valid meditative vision.

The appearance of Piers as like Christ, finally, supports the whole argument. Piers has been approached by scholars in many ways, all of which have enlarged the mystery of his function in the poem.[19] The best way to understand him, I am convinced, is to see that his function in *Piers Plowman* is equivalent to that of the Bride of Christ in Bernard's sermons on the *Canticle of Canticles*, or in the many other commentaries on the *Canticle* which interpret it mystically. In Bernard's commentary, the Bride is a symbol of both the individual soul and the aggregate of souls that constitute the Mystical Body:

Take heed that you bring chaste ears to this discourse of love; and when you think of these two who are its subject, remember always that not a man and a woman are to be thought of, but the Word of God and the devout soul. And if I shall speak of Christ and the Church, the sense is the same, except that under the name of the Church is specified not one soul only, but the unity, or rather the unanimity, of many souls.[20]

In other works besides his Sermons on the *Canticle* Bernard consistently employs the Bride image in this double sense. Thus, in one of his other sermons, he says:

And the Bride? We ourself, my brethren, are the Bride, incredible though it may seem to you; we are all, collectively, one same Bride

---

[18]   Chapter LXXXI, in Migne, *P. L.*, vol. 196, coll. 57B-58A.

[19]   See Frank, *op. cit.*, 13-15, for both a summary list of interpretations of Piers and for Burdach's interpretation that Frank adopts.

[20]   Sermon LXI, 2, on the *Canticle*.

of the one Christ, and, moreover, our several souls are, so to speak, several Brides.[21]

Like the Bride, Piers is also a symbol of both the individual soul and the Church. And just as Bernard's Bride moves freely from symbolizing one to symbolizing the other, so Piers alternates between these two significances without warning. Most of the time he symbolizes a single soul, but sometimes, as he obviously does in *Dobest* (XXII:258-336), where the Paraclete makes Piers "my procuratour and my reue" (XXII:258), he symbolizes the Mystical Body and takes on the characteristics of its earthly founder. Piers also symbolizes the Church at the end of the *Visio*, where he receives the first of two pardons granted him in this poem. Allegorically the pardon is God's promise to man offered through the intermediary of the Church; literally the pardon is an indulgence which the Church may grant because as the Bride of Christ, the Mystical Body of which Christ is the head, the Church has the power to draw upon its Treasury of merits. Taken literally or allegorically, the pardon is sent specifically to Piers, and its benefits distributed by Piers to other souls because he is the Church, the intermediary between God and man.[22]

The Bride symbolizes both the individual soul and the Church, more-over, in a state of ideal perfection by which each enjoys on earth an ideal union with Christ. She acts as the universal model of a theoretical degree of perfection that the soul or the Church may achieve on earth, as distinct from the diversified and always qualified perfection that actual men and the historical Church enjoy according to the concrete conditions of their existence. The Bride presents a standard that is un-

[21] Second Sermon for the First Sunday after the Octave of the Epiphany, in *Sermons*, II, p. 44.
[22] This accounts for a small change made in the B and C-versions as compared to the A. In all three texts the Pardon is said to come from Truth to Piers. The A-text, however, says the pope has allowed other men to share in Piers's Pardon. This seems to distinguish the pope from the Church, represented by Piers. But the B-text substitutes *treuthe* for *pope* (VII:8), and the C-text substitutes the pronoun *he*, the antecedent of which is *Treuthe* (X:8). Thus the confusing, inaccurate, and possibly inflammatory detail is eliminated in the later versions.

reachable, because perfection is inexhaustible, and after which St. Bernard himself, his audience, and all souls, described as her maidens or daughters, are endlessly to strive. And as the model of the perfect lover of Christ, she is the model of all the obligations of the perfect as well as all the privileges. Thus she is depicted not only as enjoying contemplation, but also as accepting with joy the obligation of being Christ's co-worker and servant in the salvation of other souls. She returns to her maidens in order to teach them the way to Christ's abode, to encourage them, console them, and convert them because it is her beloved's will that she perform works of spiritual labor on behalf of men.[23] She is, in short, the forerunner of souls on their way to Christ.

Similarly, Piers is Langland's model and highest norm. It is for this reason that he gives the poem its title and can be said to be the subject of Will's vision. Piers is ideal earthly perfection that, because it is always beyond what can actually be achieved in this life, is a standard that can only be envisioned. Like that of the Bride, his function is to draw souls, as individuals and as members of the Mystical Body, forward to ever greater perfection by example and by effort on their behalf. Piers explains himself in his very first speech (VIII:182-203). That he has already reached perfection and now lives the Unitive Life is evinced by his claim to know Truth "as kyndeliche . as clerkus don hure bokes" (VIII:183). Conscience and Kyndewit, he says, directed him to Truth's dwelling and since that time have made him serve Truth for ever. He goes on to characterize himself as the servant of Truth, which the perfect man is qualified to become, and offers to show other souls the way. The passage ends by his refusing to take meed for his counsel, thus emphasizing that in Piers there is no trace of self-love, but a will that desires only what God desires. All his actions in the poem are those of a perfect soul that has taken on gladly the obligation of being the spiritual forerunner of others souls.

As the ideal lover of Christ, the Bride possesses virtues

---

[23] Although the function of the Bride as I have described it is manifest in the entire commentary on the *Canticle,* one can get an essential idea of her function from Sermon XXIII.

ideally. These constitute her character and appearance. Her beauty consists in charity especially, since charity is the principle of perfection and the foundation of all virtues, but also in righteousness, patience, poverty, and fear of the Lord. Prudence, temperance, fortitude, and other virtues are pearls in her coronet,[24] modesty is the color of her cheeks,[25] intelligence is her neck,[26] and so on. Most of all, because she is the image of God and contemplatively united with him, she bears in herself attributes which belong to God:

From the attributes, then, which belong to God, she justly and confidently infers that by Him whom she loves, she is herself beloved. This is, in fact, the case. The love of God for the soul produces the love of the soul for God; the direction of the Divine thought upon a soul causes that soul to direct itself towards God, and His care and solicitude in it towards Him. For, I know not by what affinity of nature it takes place, that when a soul has once attained to behold, with unveiled face, the glory of the Lord, it is speedily, as if by a necessary law, conformed to it, and transformed into the same image. God will then appear towards you, such as you shall have appeared towards Him. With an upright man (says the Psalmist) He will show Himself upright; with the pure He will show Himself pure (Ps. xviii, 25, 26). Why not, then, also loving with who loves Him, attentive with the attentive, careful with the careful, and at leisure with the leisurely?[27]

Pier's appearance and character also manifest the virtues that he possesses. Like the Bride, he is God's perfect lover and beloved, the archetype of the soul united with God in the bond of charity. In seeking Piers Plowman, the soul seeks charity. As there is a progressive simplification toward charity as the single guiding virtue in the spiritual life, so Will becomes more and more devoted to Piers as the poem progresses, shedding concern for other virtues along the way, until in the end his entire quest is reduced to the single necessity of seeking and having Piers Plowman, love of God, who will destroy pride, the love of self that is the arch-enemy in the Unitive Life:

[24] *Ibid.,* Sermon XXVII, 3.
[25] *Ibid.,* Sermon XL, 1.
[26] *Ibid.,* Sermon XLI, 1.
[27] *Ibid.,* Sermon LXIX, 7.

'By Crist,' quath Conscience tho . 'ich wol by-come a
   pilgryme,
And wenden as wide . as the worlde regneth,
To seke Peers the Plouhman . that Pruyde myghte des-
   truye,
And that freres hadden a fyndynge . that for neode
   flateren,
And counterpleideth me, Conscience; . nowe Kynde me
   a-venge,
And sende me hap and hele . til ich haue Peers Plouhman!'
And suthe he gradde after grace . til ich gan a-wake.

(XXIII:380-86)

Piers has charity above all virtues, but his figure is especially
determined by the two virtues that are the principal means of
achieving perfect love of God: humility and active charity. Lang-
lang's spiritual forerunner is a plowman, I feel, not only because
such a figure serves the author's reformist purpose and the practical cast of his spirituality, but also because the plowman, as in
The Canterbury Tales, may eminently epitomize humility and
active charity. In these two virtues are contained all virtues, and
in them are contained all the characteristics that Piers bears.
He is summed up near the end of the poem by the "curatour of
holykirke", who says, "Ac wel worthe Peers Plouhman . that
porsueth god in doynge" (XXII:432), and continues:

Right so Peers Plouhman . peyneth hym to tulye
As wel for a wastour . other for a wench atte stewes,
As for hym-self and his servauns . saue he is furst
   yserued;
So blessed beo Peers Plouhman . that peyneth hym to
   tulie,
And trauaileth and tuleth . for a tretour al-so sore
As for a trewe tydy man . alle tymes ylyke.

(XXII:436-41)

In placing himself at the service even of sinners, Piers is perfect
humility; in being concerned for the good of others as for himself,
he is fraternal charity.

Piers's relationship to other souls, then, is that of forerunner,
in the broad sense of model, servant, and source of inspiration,
teaching, and example. He turns up when souls need his guidance.

In himself he is perfect from his first appearance to his last; he does not grow in spiritual perfection with each of his appearances, nor undergo a change in his spiritual condition. When he says, at the end of the B-*Visio*, for example, that he will no longer be so busy about the world (B, VII:117-29), he is not himself undergoing a change of heart, for in heart he is already permanently bound to Truth. The C-text eliminates this speech and, along with it, possible confusion on this point. Rather, Piers seeks to produce by example a change of heart in other souls, showing them the need voluntarily to accept poverty of spirit.[28] But while Piers does not change in his spiritual nature, he does change in his dramatic function, because, as forerunner, he responds to the soul's need and thus reflects the condition of the soul he is guiding at the point at which his guidance is necessary. Thus in passus 9 of the Visio, he is first a pilgrim, then a plowman, then an old man (IX:56-111), taking on the characteristics his proteges must take on if they are to move forward toward the perfection Piers already enjoys. His dramatic appearances are determined by the souls he is guiding rather than by his own spiritual nature. Or, to re-state this from another point of view, the way Piers is seen and understood is determined by the degree of spiritual progress reached by other souls, according to the principle behind deification that only like knows like.

As Will, the representative soul, grows spiritually, he also grows in understanding of Piers as being perfect: that is, as "a god on earth and like our Lord". His devotion to Piers becomes increasingly intense because his understanding of Piers grows, and his understanding grows as he, himself, approaches spiritual perfection. Will finally sees Piers in his naked perfection, so to speak, in passus 22:

---

[28] Another reason for eliminating the *ne solliciti sitis* speech from the B-version is that while Piers is always ahead of his flock, at this point he is too far ahead. The soul is not prepared to accept poverty until it has humbled itself completely, and this is not achieved until passus 17, just before the appearance of *Liberum Arbitrium*. The *ne solliciti sitis* speech makes a poor transition to *Dowel* because it looks forward to the end of *Dowel* rather than its beginning. From the point of view of spiritual progress, the C-*Visio* has a better ending than the B-*Visio* has.

> Ich fel eft-sones a-slepe . and sodeynliche me mette,
> That Peers the Plouhman . was peynted al blody,
> And cam yn with a croys . by-fore the comune peuple,
> And ryght like in alle lymes . to our lord Iesu;
> And thenne calde ich Conscience . to kenne me the sothe.
> 'Is this Iesus the Iouster?' quath ich . 'that Iuwes duden
>   to deathe,
> Other is hit Peers Plouhman? . ho peynted hym so rede?'
> Quath Conscience, and kneolede tho . 'these aren Christes
>   armes,
> Hus colours and hus cote-armure . and he that cometh so
>   blody,
> Hit is Crist with his crois . conqueror of Crystine.'

> (XXII:5-14)

This passage, which duplicates the corresponding passage in B (XIX:5-14) practically word for word, makes it clear that Piers is not identical with Christ in substance, but "ryght like in alle lymes . to oure lord Iesu". If Langland meant Piers to be Christ, either in Christ's human nature or in his divine nature, he would not introduce confusion about the likeness between them.[29] Piers now manifests himself in his very perfection, as bearing, according to Lady Church's teaching and the doctrine of deification, the likeness of God. He is "Cristes armes, / Hus colours and hus cote-armure" not only because he is human nature perfected, but also because he is humility and charity, the virtues that Hilton calls Christ's livery, that he says arrays the soul in Christ's likeness, and in virtue of which Christ knows the soul intimately and shows himself to it.[30] Will is able to see the deified Piers because he is now like Piers. He, himself, has achieved perfection, and at this moment he is experiencing comtemplation. It would have been difficult, if not impossible, for Langland to show Will as

[29] Such passages as the "*Petrus, id est, Christus*" passage, which prompt us to view Piers as a symbol of Christ rather than a soul like Christ, are mainly found in the B-text and eliminated in the C. I think Langland struck them out because of their undesirable implications. They not only be-cloud the role of Piers, but also smack of monism. By cancelling them, Langland both clarified his plowman and prevented the possible charge of heresy. Again I agree with Donaldson that while the B-version may have some better poetry than the C has, the C-version has more precise theology.

[30] *Scale*, I, 51, p. 81.

being like Christ and to have Will present himself in a mystic state. Instead, Langland reveals Piers as deified, allowing the very fact that Will can now see Piers in this way to speak for Will's own experience. By now, therefore, Will has achieved the goal he has sought from the beginning, and the spiritual teaching of *Piers Plowman* has been fulfilled.

SELECTED BIBLIOGRAPHY

Aquinas, Saint Thomas, *Apology for the Religious Orders*. Trans. The Very Rev. Father John Procter, S.T.M. (London, Sands & Co, 1902).
——, *The Commandments of God: Conferences on the Two Precepts of Charity and the Ten Commandments*. Trans. Laurence Shapcote, O.P. (London, Burns Oates & Washbourne Ltd., 1937).
——, *The Religious State, the Episcopate, and the Priestly Office: A translation of the minor work of the Saint on the Perfection of the Spiritual Life*. The very Rev. Father Procter, S.T.M. (Maryland, The Newman Press, 1950).
——, *The Summa Theologica*. Trans. The Fathers of the English Dominican Province, 21 vols. (London, Burns Oates & Washbourne, Ltd., 1911-1923).
Bernard of Clairvaux, Saint, *Concerning Grace and Free Will*. Trans. Watkin Williams (New York, The Macmillan Co., 1920).
——, *The Letters of St. Bernard of Clairvaux*. Trans. Bruno Scott James (Chicago, Henry Regnery Company, 1953).
——, *Life and Works of Saint Bernard*, Vol. IV. Trans. Samuel J. Eales (London, 1896).
——, *Of Conversion*. Trans. Watkin Williams (London, Burns Oates & Washbourne, 1938).
——, *On Consideration*. Trans. A Priest of Mount Melleray (Dublin, Browne and Nolan Ltd., 1921).
——, *On the Love of God (De Diligendo Deo)*. Trans. A Religious of C.S.M.V. (London, A. R. Mowbray & Co., 1950).
——, *Sermons for the Seasons and Principal Festivals of the Year*. Trans. A Priest of Mount Melleray. 3 vols. (Westminster, Md., The Carroll Press, 1950).
——, *The Steps of Humility*. Trans. George Bosworth Burch (Cambridge, Mass., Harvard University Press, 1942).
Bloomfield, Morton W., *Piers Plowman as a Fourteenth-Century Apocalypse* (New Brunswick, N.J., Rutgers University Press, n.d. [1962]).
——, "Present State of *Piers Plowman* Studies", *Speculum*, XIV (1939), 215-32.
Butler, Dom Cuthbert, *Western Mysticism: The Teaching of SS. Augustine, Gregory and Bernard on Contemplation and the Contemplative Life*, 2nd ed., with "Afterthoughts" (London, Constable, 1951).

Chambers, Raymond W., *Man's Unconquerable Mind: Studies of English Writers, from Bede to A. E. Housman and W. P. Ker* (London, Jonathan Cape, 1939).

The Cloud of Unknowing and the Book of Privy Counselling. Ed. Phyllis Hodgson, *EETS,* CCXVIII (1944).

The Cloud of Unknowing and Other Treatises by an English Mystic of the Fourteenth Century: With a Commentary on the Cloud by Father Augustine Baker, O.S.B. Ed. Abbot Justin McCann, 6th ed. (Westminster, Md., The Newman Press, 1952).

Coghill, Nevill I., "The Character of Piers Plowman Considered from the B-Text", *Medium Aevum,* II (1933), 108-35.

——, "The Pardon of Piers Plowman", *Proceedings of the British Academy,* XXX (1944), 303-57.

Colledge, Eric, *The Mediaeval Mystics of England* (New York, Charles Scribner's Sons, 1961).

Courcelle, Pierre, "Tradition neo-platonicienne et traditions Chrétiennes de la 'région de dissemblance' ". *Archives d'histoire doctrinale et littéraire du Moyen Age,* XXIV (1957), 5-33.

Dawson, Christopher, *Medieval Religion.* The Forwood Lectures, 1934 (London, Sheed and Ward, 1935).

Denise Hid Diuinite and Other Treatises on Contemplative Prayer Related to The Cloud of Unknowing: A tretyse of þe Stodye of Wysdome þat Men Clepen Beniamyn; A Pistle of Preier; A Pistle of Discrecioun. Ed. Phyllis Hodgson. *EETS,* vol. 231 (London, 1955).

Donaldson, E. Talbot, *Piers Plowman: the C-text and Its Poet* (New Haven, Yale University Press, 1949).

Dunning T. P., *Piers Plowman: An Interpretation of the A-text* (London, Longmans, Green & Co., 1937).

——, "The Structure of the B-Text", *Review of English Studies,* N.S., VII (1956), 225-37.

Erzgräber, Willi, *William Langlands Piers Plowman (Eine Interpretation des C-Textes)* (= *Frankfurter Arbeiten aus dem Gebiete der Anglistik und der Amerika-Studien,* Heft III) (Heidelberg, Carl Winter Universitätsverlag, 1957).

Fowler, David C., *Piers the Plowman: Literary Relations of the A and B Texts* (Seattle, University of Washington Press, 1961).

Frank, Robert Worth, Jr., "The Art of Reading Medieval Personification Allegory", *English Literary History,* XX (1953), 237-50.

——, *Piers Plowman and the Scheme of Salvation: An Interpretation of Dowel, Dobet, and Dobest* (New Haven, Yale University Press, 1957).

Garrigou-Lagrange, Rev. Reginald, O.P., *Christian Perfection and Contemplation According to St. Thomas Aquinas and St. John of the Cross.* Trans. Sister M. Timothea Doyle, O.P. (St. Louis, B. Herder Book Co., 1951).

Gilson, Etienne, *History of Christian Philosophy in the Middle Ages* (New York, Random House, 1955).

——, *The Mystical Theology of Saint Bernard.* Trans. A. H. C. Downes (London and New York, Sheed and Ward, 1940).

——, "Regio Dissimilitudinis de Platon a St. Bernard de Clairvaux", *Mediaeval Studies,* IX (1947), 108-30.

——, *The Spirit of Mediaeval Philosophy.* Trans. A. H. C. Downes (New York, Scribners, 1940).

——, *Théologie et Histoire de la Spiritualité* (Paris, Librairie Philosophique J. Vrin, 1943).

Hilton, Walter, *The Goad of Love.* Ed. Clare Kirchberger (London, Faber and Faber Ltd., 1952).

——, *The Scale of Perfection.* Trans. Dom Gerard Sitwell (London, Burns Oates, 1953).

Horstman, C., Yorkshire Writers: *Richard Rolle of Hampole, An English Father of the Church, and His Followers* (London, Swan Sonnenschein & Co., 1895).

Hort, Greta, *Piers Plowman and Contemporary Religious Thought* (London, Society for Promoting Christian Knowledge, n. d.).

Hulbert, J. R., "*Piers the Plowman* after Forty Years", *Modern Philology,* XLV (1948), 215-25.

Inge, William Ralph, *Christian Mysticism,* 8th ed. (London, Methuen & Co. Ltd., 1948).

Julian of Norwich, *Revelation of Divine Love* (London, Thomas Richardson and Sons, 1877).

Jusserand, J. J., *Piers Plowman, A Contribution to the History of English Mysticism.* Revised and Enlarged by the Author. Trans. M. E. R. (London, T. Risher Unwin, 1894).

Kane, George, *Middle English Literature: A critical Study of the Romances, the Religious Lyrics, Piers Plowman* (London, Methuen & Co., 1951).

Kempe, Margery, *The Book of Margery Kempe.* Ed. Sanford Brown Meech and Hope Emily Allen (= *EETS,* vol 212) (London, Oxford University Press, 1940).

Knowles, David, *The English Mystics* (New York, Benziger Brothers, 1927).

——, *The English Mystical Tradition* (New York, Harper, 1961).

Langland, William, *Piers the Plowman: A Critical Edition of the A-Version.* Ed. Thomas A. Knott and David C. Fowler (Baltimore, The John Hopkins Press, 1952).

——, *The Vision of William Concerning Piers the Plowman in Three Parallel Texts together with Richard the Redeless.* Ed. Rev. W. W. Skeat, 2 vols. (Oxford, Clarendon Press, 1886).

——, *Will's Visions of Piers Plowman and Do-Well.* Ed. George Kane (University of London, The Athlone Press, 1960).

Lawlor, John, *Piers Plowman: An Essay in Criticism* (New York, Barnes & Noble, Inc., 1962).

Lewis, C. S., *The Allegory of Love: A Study in Medieval Tradition* (London, Oxford University Press, 1938).

Maisack, Helmut, *William Langlands Verhältnis zum Zisterziensischen Mönchtum: Eine Untersuchung der Vita im Piers Plowman.* Tübingen Inaugural Dissertation (Balingen, Hermann Daniel, 1953).

Mensendieck, Otto, "The Authorship of *Piers Plowman*", *Journal of English and Germanic Philology,* IX (1910), 404-20.

Meroney, Howard, "The Life and Death of Longe Wille", *A Journal of English Literary History*, XVII (1950), 1-35.

Molinari, Paul, *Julian of Norwich: The Teaching of a 14th Century English Mystic* (London, Longmans, Green and Co., 1958).

Owst, G. R., *Literature and Pulpit in Medieval England, a Neglected Chapter in the History of English Letters & of the English People* (Cambridge, University Press, 1933).

——, *Preaching in Medieval England: An Introduction to Sermon Manuscripts of the Period c. 1350-1450* (Cambridge, University Press, 1926).

Parente, Pascal P., *The Ascetical Life* (St. Louis, Mo., B. Herder Book Co., 1945).

——, *The Mystical Life* (St. Louis, Mo., B. Herder Book Co., 1946).

Pepler, Conrad, O.P., *The English Religious Heritage* (St. Louis, B. Herder Book Co., 1958).

Pourrat, P., *Christian Spirituality*. Trans. W. H. Mitchell, 4 vols. (New York, P. J. Kenedy, 1924).

Robertson, D. W. Jr. and Huppé, Bernard, *Piers Plowman and Scriptural Tradition* (= *Princeton Studies in English*, No. 31) (Princeton, University Press, 1951).

Rolle, Richard, *English Writings of Richard Rolle, Hermit of Hampole*. Ed. Hope Emily Allen (Oxford, Clarendon Press, 1931).

Salter, Elizabeth, *Piers Plowman: An Introduction* (Cambridge, Mass., Harvard University Press, 1962).

Sitwell, Gerard, *Spiritual Writers of the Middle Ages* (New York, Hawthorn Books, 1961).

Taylor, Henry Osborn, *The Medieval Mind: A History of the Development of Thought and Emotion in the Middle Ages*, 4th ed., 2 vols. (London, Victor Gollancz Ltd., 1951).

Traver, Hope, *The Four Daughters of God: A Study of the Versions of this Allegory with especial reference to those in Latin, French, and English* (Philadelphia, John C. Winston Co., 1907).

Underhill, Evelyn, *Mysticism: A Study in the Nature and Development of Man's Spiritual Consciousness*, 4th ed. (London, Methuen & Co., 1912).

Vernet, Felix, *La Spiritualité Medievale* (= *Bibliothèque Catholique des Sciences Religieuses*, Vol. 21) (Librairie Bloud & Gay, 1929).

Wells, Henry W., "The Construction of *Piers Plowman*", *Publications of the Modern Language Association*, XLIV (1929), 123-40.

——, "The Philosophy of *Piers Plowman*", *Publications of the Modern Language Association*, LIII (1938), 339-49.

Zeeman, Elizabeth, "Piers Plowman and the Pilgrimage to Truth", *Essays and Studies*, N. S., XI (1958), 1-16.

STUDIES IN ENGLISH LITERATURE

Out:

1. William H. Matchett: *The Phoenix and the Turtle. Shakespeare's Poem and Chester's Loues Martyr.* 1965. 213 pp. Cloth.   Gld. 26.—

2. Ronald David Emma: *Milton's Grammar.* 1964. 164 pp.   Gld. 18.—

3. George A. Panichas: *Adventure in Consciousness. The Meaning of D. H. Lawrence's Religious Quest.* 1964. 225 pp., portrait.   Gld. 25.—

4. Henrietta Ten Harmsel: *Jane Austen. A Study in Fictional Conventions.* 1964. 206 pp. Gld. 22.—

5. Dorothy Schuchman McCoy: *Tradition and Convention. A Study of Periphrasis in English Pastoral Poetry from 1557-1715.* 1965. 289 pp. Gld. 30.—

6. Ted E. Boyle: *Symbol and Meaning in the Fiction of Joseph Conrad.* 1965. 245 pp.   Gld. 24.—

7. Josephine O'Brien Schaefer: *The Three-Fold Nature of Reality in the Novels of Virginia Woolf.* 1965. 210 pp.   Gld. 24.—

8. Gerard Anthony Pilecki: *Shaw's "Geneva". A Critical Study of the Evolution of the Text in Relation to Shaw's Political Thought and Dramatic Practice.* 1965. 189 pp.   Gld. 20.—

MOUTON & CO. • PUBLISHERS • THE HAGUE